STRANGERS AND PILGRIMS ONCE MORE

STRANGERS AND PILGRIMS ONCE MORE

Being Disciples of Jesus in a Post-Christendom World

ADDISON HODGES HART

WILLIAM B. EERDMANS PUBLISHING COMPANY
Grand Rapids, Michigan / Cambridge, U.K.

WM. B. EERDMANS PUBLISHING CO.
2140 Oak Industrial Drive N.E., Grand Rapids, Michigan 49505 /
P.O. Box 163, Cambridge CB3 9PU U.K.
www.eerdmans.com

Printed in the United States of America

20 19 18 17 16 15 14   7 6 5 4 3 2 1

Library of Congress Cataloging-in-Publication Data

ISBN 978-0-8028-6974-6

Unless otherwise noted, the Scripture quotations in this publication are from
the Revised Standard Version of the Bible, copyrighted 1946, 1952 © 1971, 1973
by the Division of Christian Education of the National Council of Churches of
Christ in the U.S.A., and used by permission.

Dedicated to my "fellow disciples":

My brother, Robert W. Hart, II,
Martin D. Eppard,
Jeffrey J. Atherholt,
and
Jerome J. Atherholt.

*We have traveled along different
paths from whence we set out;
but, though often separated,
we remain inseparable in Christ.*

CONTENTS

vii

INTRODUCTION: LIVING AS DISCIPLES IN A DYING CHRISTENDOM

"Ἀγαπητοί, παρακαλῶ ὡς παροίκους καὶ παρεπιδήμους ἀπέχεσθαι τῶν σαρκικῶν ἐπιθυμιῶν αἵτινες στρατεύονται κατὰ τῆς ψυχῆς . . ."

"Dearly beloved, I beseech you as strangers and pilgrims, abstain from fleshly lusts, which war against the soul . . ."

"Beloved, I beseech you as aliens and exiles to abstain from the passions of the flesh that wage war against your soul."

1 Peter 2:11 (Greek original; KJV; RSV)

I.

This is a book of oppositions. Everything I discuss in the following pages is set in the framework of "Yes and No" — *sic et non.* Primarily, it is a book opposing Christianity to Christendom, or, at least, recognizing them as different and even often at odds in both basic principles and practical results — in both their roots and their fruits, to use the language of Pragmatism.

It's also a book of sketches. Like someone sketching pictures in a sketch pad, I wish only to delineate, shape, and shade a few aspects of Christianity. These are quick studies only, not full portraits. Still, these aspects are important ones for Christians, each one indispensable to discipleship. Each chapter will be an unembellished outline of what I imagine these aspects of Christianity must become in the wake of Christendom.

By the term "Christendom" I mean any alliance of church and state that can trace its historical roots all the way back to Constantine in the fourth century, tributary though it may be. Further, I mean the West, and European culture in particular. By "European culture" I mean not only Europe itself, but also the United States, Australia, and other extensions of Christendom throughout the world. (For those Europeans who might wish it were otherwise, it's important that they be reminded that the United States is a cultural continuation of themselves. When they look at the United States and dislike what they see, what they see is only a slightly exaggerated reflection of their own faces peering back at them. All the imperialism, colonialism, violent tendencies, racism, brashness, hubris, and hawkishness they disdain at times in Americans came directly from Caucasian Europe; just as many things that are good about America are European as well.)

The process of Christendom's disintegration began a long while ago, continues apace, and appears to be irreversible. All the constituents of Christian life which I will discuss in the pages that follow (such as dogma, the Bible, sacraments, and so on) have undergone external changes before, and they have been challenged perennially by the strains of both development and corruption throughout Christianity's history ever since. The questions before us now are how they will manage in a post-Christendom context, and how Christians might best preserve their permanent meanings in an age marked by decidedly post- (if not anti-) Christian cultural norms. Those are the implicit inquiries I have in mind as I attempt each sketch.

II.

The single sentence that heads this introduction provides the moral premise of this book. It is taken from a first-century epistle, one of two ascribed to the apostle Peter, addressed to "strangers" or "exiles" *(parepidemois)* who lived in regions which today belong to Turkey, but were at the time provinces of the Roman Empire (1 Pet. 1:1). I have presented the text in three versions, including the Greek original; but if I were to render it into English myself, my version would read, "Beloved, I exhort you as strangers and pilgrims, abstain from fleshly passions, which war against your life."

Now, most English translations render the word I would translate as "life" *(psyche)* as "soul." I like the word "soul," and use it when I refer to a personal life vibrant with intellect, subtlety, and sensibility. But I also think the word carries some acquired philosophical and theological baggage that's misleading. The "soul" is often thought of as an immaterial element that indwells and propels our bodies — the familiar "ghost in the machine." We sometimes forget that the Greek word *psyche* simply means "life," and it is inextricably associated with all things bodily. It doesn't refer only to human life; it might just as well refer to the life of a cricket or a buffalo or a melon or any other living thing. Literally, the word has to do with breathing, which even vegetation must do after its kind. So *psyche* in our text above means concrete, daily, earthly human life — not a "substance" as such, not a *thing* that *is not* our bodies, or doesn't include our bodies, or indwells our bodies like a genie corked inside a bottle until the day it's released. No; *psyche* means our whole being, including our bodies and their senses.

Whenever I walk up the mountain trail near my home in Norway, as I did this morning, breathing in the clean winter air, looking through the trees out over the fjord toward the mountains and the glacier beyond, listening to the sounds of birds, and invariably throwing sticks for my dog to chase — it is my "soul" that is doing all these physical and sensual things. When I return home and eat breakfast, when I kiss my wife Good Morning, when I burn my tongue with the hot coffee — it is my "soul" that eats and kisses and gets a burned tongue. However, a more sensible and pragmatic way of putting all this is to say that these things are part of *life*. If I put it like that, I can bring the meaning down to earth where it belongs.

I want to begin, then, by affirming simply that living life is its own meaning. Some Christians may balk at that statement; but if we should pause and reflect for a moment, we would have to say that "life" is placed right at the heart of Christian faith. "Eternal life" may be life magnified and extended and vaster than what we presently experience; but even "eternal life" for us begins right here with the simple existence we possess now. I will go a step further and say that our own personal lives are the most precious possessions we have. If we think that that's a selfish attitude, we should recall the supreme importance Jesus placed on these lives of ours. After telling us that we should "lose" our life *(psyche)* for his sake — that is to say, be willing to give him our all — he then told us in effect that each one of us should place immense value on those same individual lives: "For what does it profit a man, to gain the whole world and forfeit his life? For what can a man give in return for his life?" (Mark 8:36-37). In other words, each of us should regard and treat our life as infinitely precious — greater even than possession of "the whole world." We are not to sell our selves cheaply. If we should ever sacrifice the life we have, we had better be sure it's for the right reasons.

The question we can then ask ourselves is whether or not we're living our lives well or poorly. Our text in 1 Peter tells us straightforwardly that "fleshly passions" are in actual fact what make our lives difficult. "Fleshly" might be understood as meaning a predominant focus on our *selves,* regardless of whether or not they inconvenience or harm or objectify others — "selfish" in the most self-serving, "me"-centered, self-"pleasuring" sense. The Greek word for "passions," of course, covers a lot of ground in the New Testament wherever it appears, and it frequently means "wrong desires" (misdirected sexual lust is only one among the many wrong desires we house within ourselves). Without a doubt, "fleshly passions" refers to those inner dispositions that lead us into acts of greed, theft, mendacity, violence, coarseness, callousness, hatred, hubris, anger, and misdirected sexual lust. These come from within and poison our invaluable lives (cf. Mark 7:20-23).

But, having once acknowledged that our passions spring from within us, often to our detriment, we need to turn our attention to the terms with which the epistle addresses its readers: "I exhort you," it reads, "as strangers and pilgrims." If the phrase "fleshly passions" turns us inward to see what's tugging at us from inside, the phrase "strangers and pilgrims" reminds us that outside ourselves we also have forces that tug at us constantly and make unwarranted demands on our attention.

What do these words, then, imply?

The word "strangers" means that the epistle's readers are expected to view themselves as aliens — "resident aliens," as others have noted. "Resident aliens" live in one country but are citizens of another. For instance, I reside in Norway, although I am an American citizen. In Norway, then, I am a resident alien, a stranger in their midst.

The Greek word translated as "pilgrims" has sometimes been translated as "exiles." Either way, it means those who are passing to or from a place. I prefer the word "pilgrims" as a translation of the Greek *parepidemois* because it suggests that the readers should see themselves as those passing through one region to reach another. Along these lines, I am reminded of one of the sayings of Jesus in the *Gospel of Thomas* (an unquestionably early Christian gospel, it should be noted, which can be read in a far less "unorthodox" way than it is often presented). In one brief, blunt line, Jesus austerely says to his followers, "Become passers-by" (logion 42). It's an obscure command. There is no elaboration of it in the text; but I think I can guess its meaning well enough. It seems likely that it is an authentic saying of Jesus. But, even if it is not, it has perennial meaning. It reminds us that we are pilgrims and that we are just passing through. And it is as applicable for us today as for those early disciples of Jesus.

III.

I write as an American Christian, a native and citizen of the world's latest, greatest superpower. I write under no illusions about the fact that the United States is an expanding militaristic empire, the most recent in a long line of empires that have been born, have expanded and contracted, and have then died out as empires, even if they have continued to exist in some reduced national form. Nor do I doubt for an instant that there existed once a nobler, old-fashioned American character, but it has changed drastically for the worse since the Second World War (although, I could argue, if this were a book about American history, that the national character was already in decline a full century before that). Perhaps we saw it most starkly in a series of events: first, in the country's reactions to Communist expansion, followed (in fatal connection, really, to the first) by its ill-advised wars "on terror." In point of fact, America has been in a nearly constant state of war since 1941 (though, again, one could make a strong case that this began much earlier), and today the number of U.S. military bases globally is estimated by some to be in the vicinity of seven hundred, by others to number more than one thousand.

Furthermore, despite the rhetoric — real and feigned — about faith that one hears in the public square, American Christians should be quick to note that the national, serviceable, civil version of Christianity bears almost no discernible relation, beyond misapplied quotations, to the actual teachings of Jesus. Jesus Christ is always good, in other words, for an inspirational sound bite. The United States is one of the last great Western powers to employ "Christendom" language deliberately to defend its ideas of freedom, economics, democracy, and war (always war), regardless of its vaunted church-state separateness. But, notwithstanding the loud and showy religiosity of politicians at election time, and despite the determined efforts of an activist Christian fundamentalism "at the heart of American power" (to borrow the phrase used in the subtitle of Jeff Sharlet's unnerving book *The Family*), American culture is nevertheless a *post-Christendom* culture, openly espousing a host of practical values that an older, pre-modern Christendom would have rightly condemned as vices (because they cater to those "fleshly passions" mentioned above). Any culture, for instance, that upholds as its exemplars those who declare — or more privately act upon an opinion — that *greed* is a "good" is a culture that is conspicuously "post-Christendom" (and post-Christian). Only a pretense of Christian values remains.

So, then, in what way are followers of Jesus to be *passers-by* — strangers and pilgrims — in such a context?

The answer should be increasingly obvious to today's thinking Christians — *should be,* I say, though it often doesn't look like it is. Modestly put, if we seek to follow Jesus, we must be passers-by of many things around us: we should keep alert, we should discern where we are, we ought at times to avoid and not touch; we shouldn't condemn, but neither should we be duped or gullible or willing to buy the latest cultural dope on offer; we should just move along, behaving circumspectly and speaking up when necessary — boldly, charitably, humbly — and hope that our dissimilarity from many societal norms will testify to others that there exists a better, more peaceable, more loving way to live. To each one of us, as to Jesus, the words from the book of Isaiah should apply: "He will not wrangle or cry aloud, nor will any one hear his voice in the streets; he will not break a bruised reed or quench a smoldering wick, till he brings justice to victory" (Matt. 12:19-20; see Isa. 42:1-4, 9). We are to be strangers or aliens, pilgrims or exiles, and not regard ourselves as *fully identified* ethically or philosophically with our present age, society, nation, or culture. *Partially,* perhaps; but *not fully.* Of course, we participate in society, but only — ethically speaking — to a point, and always with the vivid awareness that we're passers-by.

We should be prepared to embrace this uncomfortable, unsettled way of thinking for the reason hinted at in our text from 1 Peter above: because, if we don't adopt this mode of thinking and living as Christ's disciples, we may find ourselves compromising our most cherished principles. It's the tar-baby effect — we don't stop along the way and begin a sticky interaction. Our "fleshly passions" are too easily swayed by the wrong stimuli; and there are always ample sources for sleazy suasion in the ages and nations and societies and cultures of humankind. The apostle Paul put a similar warning to Christians in this manner: "Do not be conformed to this world [*aion* = "age"], but be transformed by the renewal of your mind" (Rom. 12:2). We should develop the mental art of knowing how to pass through our age with grace and dignity. We should ever be learning to be prudent passers-by

8

and pilgrims, with a relaxed, elegant, skilled, and gently cautious practice. There should be a "Zen" quality to our discipleship, a sort of dispassionate proficiency that we cultivate over time, without giving up on our practice when we fall short (as we will from time to time). We shouldn't be fearful and fretful over our lives, or even over our sins (the word "sin" merely means "falling short," after all), but confident and unperturbed as we keep moving on in our pilgrimage — at least to the extent that our day-to-day circumstances permit us a trouble-free passage.

None of this is to say that we are to despise our native land. Patriotism has its place, so long as it is affection for one's heritage and not chauvinism. One can love one's nation and support it within reasonable limits without giving it primary allegiance. Primary allegiance for the follower of Christ belongs to God and his kingdom (cf. Matt. 6:33). Culture surely can be appreciated for its healthy achievements, its arts enjoyed, its sciences engaged, and we can enjoy the benefits of participation in society without undue anxiety. Nothing I've written here is meant to imply that we're to become "strangers" in the sense of becoming merely strange. But it does mean that we must be willing not to cling to cultural things and societal standards; to see them as possibly dispensable, always temporary, and not the goal or destination of our pilgrimage. We will leave all earthly things behind soon enough as it is.

We are passing, each of us, through our own individual lives, and we shall all let go of everything in time. Our lives, our "psyches," as we noted earlier, must come first in our consideration: What is best for the life we have each been given? How do we keep it and not forfeit it? When we read in Colossians 3:3 that we "have died" and our "life is hid with Christ in God," this seemingly dire pronouncement should be taken only as a sobering reminder. Our tents are pitched here for just a little while, and then — whoosh — we aren't here any longer. We're dead even now, says Colossians to us, even in the midst of life. We die daily. In a flash we will move on, ready or not. To say that we "have died" with Christ (in baptism sacramentally, but also as a set frame of mind) is to remind ourselves of the brevity of earthly existence. We are passers-by by nature, not by faith only. We are strangers and pilgrims because none of us — religious or non-religious or anti-religious — can abide here very long. Christians, as surely as Buddhists, are meant to live with the awareness of death daily and intimately. Our perspective is to take the longer view which Jesus proposes and "set [our] minds on things that are above" (Col. 3:2) as strangers and pilgrims here.

However much we may love, in the very best sense, our nation or culture as resident aliens, we won't be staying as permanent occupants. Nor do we yet abide in God's kingdom as fully come; rather, it abides in us in the way we are (supposed to be) living our lives. The kingdom is both here now and yet to come. Despite this, this is not really a "paradox," as some have called it; rather, it is a vital *continuity* between the indwelling presence of God's kingdom in our life now and the realized kingdom we hope ultimately to indwell. The course of our lives flows naturally toward, and so determines, our lives in God ultimately.

IV.

As stated at the outset, this book is merely a series of sketches of what being Christian might look like for us as we continue on our pilgrimage today. Once again we find ourselves in the role of "strangers and pilgrims," a role that we haven't fully experienced for the better part of 1700 years in the Western world. Eastern Christians can, of course, tell a different tale. Both Islam and

Communism took a heavy toll on the churches of the East, and these followers of Christ have known for centuries the reality of being "passers-by" in a hostile environment. There is much, I dare say, we can learn from the ordeals they experienced. I have often been struck by the sobriety, humility, and maturity of those Christians who held firm during some of the most grievous crises of the twentieth century in particular. In comparison to them, many Western Christians look lamentably soft, self-absorbed, and juvenile. That said, in the West today we are faced with a somewhat different situation than the situation of Eastern Europe, Asia, and Africa, and we must learn how to be strangers in a context also different from theirs.

In the pages ahead I will touch on a few subjects for thought. My presupposition is not that Christendom was a grave mistake and nothing more. Mistake or not, it was a historical fact. I cannot presume to say whether it was "God's will" or not; I believe only that God was no more absent from humankind in the long age of Christendom than he was before it and continues to be after it. Speaking only for myself, I find it impossible to believe that God ever had any permanent investment in Christendom at all, either in its origins or its continuance. Nor can I believe that he has conferred any special status on the United States. I say I "cannot" believe it, not that I willfully "do not" believe it; and what I mean by that is that I believe God is beyond all such human ventures. The kingdom of God is an alternative to, not a complement of, earthly power: "My kingdom is not of this world," Jesus said (John 18:36, KJV). I haven't enough "faith" to believe otherwise; and if I had, I would fear I worshiped an idol of diminutive proportions. Was Christendom a mistake? I don't know. I just know it lasted a long time, but now its time is very nearly up.

Nor do I write this without melancholy. The age of Christendom has left us with innumerable and wondrous accomplishments in virtually every field that matters (including science). When I pray vocally, I use *The Book of Common Prayer,* and when I worship, I want icons, incense, vested choirs, chanting, stained glass, grand architecture. . . . And so on. I treasure the great and wide variety of art, literature, music, and philosophy of the seventeen centuries of Christendom, from its earliest times to the present day. Ecclesiastically speaking, I love its saints and heroes; it was the age of cathedrals, monasticism, mystics, thinkers, and bold reformers. I love it all, both the heritage of East and West; and I'm in no hurry to see any of it go. But — as an epoch, and as a political force — go it shall. We can take as much of its great gifts with us as we can manage, and I hope we can manage a lot. But, Christendom or no Christendom, the kingdom of God, which Jesus preached, is still with us and still a living option; and just possibly it needed to be freed finally from the cultural constraints and numerous misconceptions that Christendom has imposed on the clear message of the good news for far too long.

The strangers and pilgrims of today are not, and cannot be, exactly like the strangers and pilgrims of the first three centuries of Christian history. We have been through too much for nearly two millennia to think that we can simply imitate the pristine, untransformed church of early Christianity. There never was a "golden age" of Christianity anyway — not the apostolic age, or the patristic era, or the medieval West, or the Byzantine East. Every age of the church has been rife with sin, stupidity, internal conflicts, and hubris. We have nothing to go back to, even if such a thing were possible. Besides, pilgrims go forward to their destination, and that hasn't changed for us since the coming of Christ.

But, at any rate, we carry with us substance we gained in the age of Christendom. What we won't have in the future is Christendom itself. What we used to rely upon was a social order that provided the semblance of Christian ideals in our culture, and could be expected at least to give them support and lip service. That social order is nearly gone, even though there are many Christians who would still attempt to revive it by political means. However, each successive generation takes it that much further out of reach of would-be restorers. The more Christendom continues to recede in time from us, the harder it is for us even to recall with clarity the principles we once shared as a people. And as the old guard dies, what replaces them are people with few cultural bearings, little historical awareness, and religious illiteracy.

So, what of those things we still possess from Christendom here and now? Some of them we can discard. They're useless. Some of them we can hold on to with gratitude. And some things require re-evaluation and renewal. We also have challenges before us as strangers and pilgrims trying to get our bearings.

In the chapters ahead I will look at five areas of concern for Christians. Four of them (from the second chapter on) are key elements of Christian life, and the ways in which these may continue in Christian communities in the future are crucial considerations. They identify us as disciples of Jesus, and how they are received and lived will, on the one hand, need to be faithful to the past, but, on the other, must not be burdened with characteristics that misrepresent God to us, and — in consequence — us to the world. Each chapter will be a thesis in response to its antithesis. Each antithesis is one that grew up within Christendom, but, for the sake of a healthier and more effective church, would best be abandoned. So, I will be asking such questions as these: Can we say yes to dogma, but no to dogmatism? Can we say yes to the Bible, but no to biblicism? Can we say yes to the unifying power of the sacraments, but no to the divisiveness of our sacramental practices? Can we say yes to evangelism, but no to counterproductive polemicism?

The five areas of concern, stated in *sic et non* juxtapositions, provide the subjects for each of the sketches that follow. They are what these sketches are meant to delineate in a rudimentary, rough, and not very exact fashion. In short, how do we go forward with the faith and heritage we have as Christians, fitted out for the age we are now entering? What should we embrace, and what should we discard?

ONE

SAYING YES TO CHRISTIANITY, AND NO TO CHRISTENDOM

*Christendom has done away with Christianity
without being quite aware of it.*

Søren Kierkegaard, *Training in Christianity*, 1850

I.

Here's the rub. Great numbers of professing Christians have been living for approximately 1700 years, no longer as strangers and pilgrims, but as native and baptized inhabitants of "Christendom." Christendom is not Christianity.

And so the time has come for me to give some definition to this word "Christendom." Christendom, as I've already suggested in passing, is to be sharply distinguished from Christianity as a faith and the church as an institution. "Christendom" is specifically a political term. It is that historical merging of an institutional church with the government of a state, the alignment of religion with politics, and the alliance of clergy with ruling powers to share in those powers. "Christendom" has an identifiable birth some three centuries after the time of Jesus. Not only is there a gap in principles between the kingdom of God, as preached by Christ, and Christendom, but there is a substantial gap in time as well. Christendom had its beginnings with events that transpired in early-fourth-century Rome, which became in consequence the legacy of Christian Europe and, in time, its colonies throughout the world (including, of course, America).

We might call this situation the "Constantinian Privilege," after the Roman emperor Flavius Valerius Aurelius Constantinus Augustus, better known to history as Constantine "the Great." In the fateful year 312, Constantine became the empire's single reigning Caesar in the decisive battle of the Milvian Bridge. According to legend, he had seen a miraculous vision that led him to accept the superiority of the Christian faith, and under the "sign" of Christ (was it a cross? or, perhaps, the *Chi Rho* — i.e., *XP* — the first two Greek letters in *Christos?*), he brought his forces to Rome and overcame Maxentius, the rival claimant to the throne. The result was that the new emperor granted legitimacy and even primacy to the formerly persecuted church. In 380 the emperor Theodosius "the Great" went even further than Constantine had done, and named the Catholic Church the only legitimate religion of the empire. With these incremental steps by the reigning powers, the church went from outlawed and persecuted (and internally divided) sect, to privileged religion, to (tragically) persecutors of imperial religion in the space of only a few decades. The first execution for heresy took place in 385 in Trier with the execution of the ascetic and preacher Priscillian and six others. And it is precisely here that one can most sharply see the crucial difference between Jesus' concept of God's kingdom and the compromised character of Christendom.

Nevertheless, even when one acknowledges that history is more often shades of gray than clearly distinguished black and white, by no means was it entirely an unmitigated disaster either for the Western world or for the church itself that Christianity became the dominant faith. Most obvious of all, the church could emerge from the horrors of persecution. And, as for Roman society, only the most "evangelistic" of secularists could possibly claim with any credibility that there were no lasting benefits for it and for Western culture in general through this surprising event. It may seem odd to us to hear that one striking result was that charity and compassion were now placed high among the virtues in Roman society, a status they hadn't enjoyed hitherto, but that was one undoubted consequence; and the practical results of this development in public moral awareness — hospitals, orphanages, distribution of food and clothing to the poor, improvements in the treatment of prisoners, and so forth — were even acknowledged by the new faith's pagan critics. All of this has been well-documented and ably defended, and it doesn't require repetition here.[1]

It may be too much to claim in our skeptical modern age that this moment in history was miraculous, but miraculous it surely looked to the eyes of numerous Christians at the time. For many, it seemed the fulfillment in history of the promise that

---

1. I can do no better in this regard than to recommend a widely acclaimed book by my own brother, David Bentley Hart, which makes the case indisputably well. The book is *Atheist Delusions: The Christian Revolution and Its Fashionable Enemies* (New Haven: Yale University Press, 2009). The title is a bit misleading, since it is not a work of contemporary apologetics. It is, in essence, an extended correction of common misconceptions, both popular and academic, of the history of Christianity and its influence on formerly pagan Western culture, and hence our own. The concluding sentence of his book might serve as a kind of jumping-off point of my own. With the fourth-century Desert Fathers' resistance to imperial encroachments on the church in mind, he writes, "It may be the case that Christians who live amid the ruins of the old Christendom — perhaps dwelling on the far-flung frontiers of a Christian civilization taking shape in other lands — will have to learn to continue the mission of their ancient revolution in the desert, to which faith has often found it necessary, at various times, to retreat."

"the kingdom of the world [would] become the kingdom of our Lord and of his Christ" (cf. Rev. 11:15).[2] Such a merging of, on the one hand, belief in divine predestination working through history, with, on the other, the goals of a this-worldly empire bent on conquest, proved a potent mix at the time. It still is a potent mix.

But, before all this, things had been drastically different. During the first three centuries of the movement's history, before Constantine, the followers of Jesus had looked upon themselves as outsiders living within the worldly societies they occupied. Part of the ethos of being a Christian had been, in fact, learning to identify oneself with a radically different "kingdom" (or, "empire") than the Roman and Asian realms he or she inhabited physically. For example, before the advent of the "Constantinian Privilege," a baptized person had been customarily expected to forgo serving in the military or as a public magistrate. To serve the ideals of the kingdom that Jesus had proclaimed put one in a position of not participating fully in the affairs of the earthly kingdom one inhabited. A Christian's public involvement was limited in his or her old this-worldly society by the governing principles of a transcendent new citizenship, by the laws of a different realm.

So, two sets of principles had been involved — those of a kingdom that conquered and ruled through might, and those of a kingdom that restrained violent passions in favor of persuasive

2. In fact, as I will mention again in Chapter Three of this book, I have wondered if the decisive factor for the insertion of the late-first-century book of Revelation into the Catholic Church's biblical canon in the fourth century, after centuries of its status as inspired scripture being a matter for dispute and often doubted, wasn't due to its being newly interpreted after Constantine's conversion. That is to say, far from its being accepted into the New Testament because of what it was understood still to predict about the future, it was now received rather as a prophecy that could be seen to be already — at least to a great extent — fulfilled in the empire's embrace of the faith.

compassion, humility, and service to all human beings, regardless of earthly borders, status, or caste. We should be absolutely clear about this right at the outset: this truly made for an uncomfortable position for those pre-Constantinian, pre-Christendom Christians to adopt, and not all those wishing to follow Jesus did it equally well. The invitation to take up the cross unequivocally meant in that early Christian context that *you really could die for the sake of this kingdom,* and, if it should come to that, it would likely be your own people who hated, imprisoned, and destroyed you in the process.

Think for a moment of the opprobrium with which an American in today's climate might, conceivably, be met if he states that he cannot in good conscience "support the troops" in, say, Afghanistan — not as individuals, but in their capacity as carrying on America's "war on terror" on foreign soil. Kick that up a few notches, and you have some idea of what it meant for Roman Christians to refuse to serve as Roman soldiers or magistrates — to refuse, in other words, to promote the empire's agenda of warfare, or to enact its laws (including the death penalty) in the name of Caesar, to say nothing of their refusal to take part in the state's sanctioned religion.

We see something of the weight of this on Christians' daily lives in 1 Corinthians 10, when Paul writes to the church in Corinth that they are not to participate in local feasts in the pagan temples there. For members of society to absent themselves from such gatherings was surely demanding and awkward, since much that was of social significance occurred in the temples. These pagan religious centers were more than meeting houses — although Paul stresses the religious aspect above all ("You cannot drink the cup of the Lord and the cup of demons" — 1 Cor. 10:21). They were also the place for social interaction, legal transactions, the striking of bargains, family gatherings, and more. To keep apart from these sites of sacrifice, society, and commerce at the time of Paul's writing was costly for one's civic reputation, if nothing else. Not long after the composition of this epistle, however, a Christian standing apart from the social norm in such a manner could find himself or herself — during the sporadic local and, eventually, empire-wide persecutions — denounced, arrested, tried, tortured, and put to death.

Becoming a follower of Jesus took one decisively outside the Roman kingdom's most firmly held beliefs about itself. Jesus' concept of the "kingdom of heaven" gave the disciple an altered vision of what a "kingdom" was in the mind of God. It called upon the disciple to renounce violence, including state-sponsored and thus religiously "sanctified" violence, and to see all human beings — Jews and Gentiles, slaves and free, males and females (cf. Gal. 3:28) — as God's beloved creatures, dignified by virtue of their being made in his image and redeemed by his Son. No Christian had permission by Christ to shed blood, even at the behest of Caesar himself. Christianity upset the old order of male domination, elevating women to equal status with men, and children (along with slaves) to eminence as models of discipleship. It included the poor alongside the rich in its ranks. It called for parity of material goods among its members and congregations. In short, it was strikingly at odds with what the word "kingdom" (i.e., "empire") meant according to contemporary Roman usage.

All this changed with the advent of the "Constantinian Privilege." Jesus' model of God's kingdom was co-opted by the Roman meaning of "kingdom," and — although Christ's principles had a transforming impact on Roman society — the ideal of the "kingdom," as Jesus himself had taught it, became inverted. Caesar assumed the role of Christ's earthly vicar (instead of — as formerly

— one falsely called "lord"), imperial Roman wars were fought under the sign of the cross (an absurd use of this previously stark symbol of defiance against Roman brutality), and — when the church had reached its apex as the sole Roman religion — it was expected that pagan Romans would follow their emperor's example and be baptized into the imperial church. To be Roman was to be Christian. To be a Roman Christian was to serve the empire faithfully: to believe as the empire believed, to fight the empire's wars, to adjudicate — if one held the post of a Roman Christian magistrate (formerly a contradiction) — the laws of the empire, even to the point of condemning prisoners to torture and death (and — most ironic, after the year 385 — one of the charges that might call for execution was "heresy" from the prevailing Christian "orthodoxy"). And so forth.

This was, as noted above, "Christendom," an amalgam of what had formerly been separate and, in first principles, originally at odds. It's not my intention here to engage in history and trace "Christendom" as a concept down through the ages, neither in its divisions into Latin West and Greek/Slavonic East, and later — in the West — into Catholicism and Protestantism, nor to discuss the relationship of Christendom to other forms of Christianity (to the Oriental churches, for example, which were deemed heterodox by the Roman-Byzantine imperial church),[3] nor to examine Christendom's dealings with Judaism within its domains, nor its conflicts with its great theocratic rival in the south and east, Islam. It's enough here to say only that the Christendom model has been with us right down to the present century. It is still the paradigm and pat-

---

3. An excellent and fascinating introduction to the Oriental churches is *The Lost History of Christianity: The Thousand-Year Golden Age of the Church in the Middle East, Africa, and Asia — and How It Died,* by Philip Jenkins (New York: HarperCollins, 2008).

tern — consciously or not — of most, if not all, of the churches in the modern age, be they Catholic, Orthodox, or Protestant. For most Christians today, the classical Christendom model — which embraces everything from the idea of a professionally schooled clergy to the architectural layouts of church buildings to the influence that particular established churches wield in a nation's politics and social mores, and more — is the given "shape" of what we mean by "church." We have lived with this for so long that another approach is almost inconceivable to us. Wherever there is a state church (for instance, the Lutheran Church in Norway or the Church of England), there we still see Christendom, albeit in contemporary cultural dress, weakened and weakening; and wherever there is a church with special influence in a nation, as is the case in most "Catholic" and many "Orthodox" countries, there is Christendom as well. To be sure, in the United States we find a strange, anomalous sort of Christendom — a kind that has no single federal- or state-sanctioned church or any particular church with special influence. But America's odd version of it is still visibly a form of Christendom, even though it is erected upon a concept of church-state separation.

II.

While acknowledging that this model has endured into the present, at the same time it also appears that Christendom is dying. In its place, at least in Europe and America, a new ethos has been evolving and has all but supplanted the old. There are numerous indications that a new, stridently non-Christian ethos is overtaking and supplanting the old, waning Christendom of the West. Examples are plentiful. Here are just a few.

THE RISE OF ATHEISTIC/ANTI-RELIGIONIST SCIENTISM

Instead of a dogmatic religion, we are witnessing the rise of a dogmatic faith in science, which some have called "scientism." In short, it is the idea that the only genuine form of "knowledge" is empirical scientific knowledge, the only viable philosophy is that which is based on a strictly materialist view of reality (in the words of the Catholic Encyclopedia, "a philosophical system which regards matter as the only reality in the world, [and] which undertakes to explain every event in the universe as resulting from the conditions and activity of matter"), and the only ethics is that which presumes these first two premises. Any idea that doesn't fit into this frankly fundamentalist creed — even if it should come from respected scientists who don't hold to the notion that philosophical materialism is the only basis for a sound epistemology — is viewed as a sort of heresy. Scientism is the elevation of a single discipline for acquiring data (the empirical scientific method) over other disciplines of inquiry. It inflates one useful methodology into an infallible authority in all matters, forgetting that "science" as generally understood is what scientists *do* and not an oracle or an intangible entity.

Now, "knowledge" has long been defined as "justifiable belief" — and it has always been assumed that the stress is on "belief," a word that means the same as "trust." Many forms of knowledge — some empirical, some intuitive, some traditional, some aesthetic, and so on — have always been considered legitimate foundations for this belief or that. "Belief" or "trust," it should hardly need be noted, implies that there is always room for additional knowledge, and therefore reconsideration of data, in virtually every field of learning.

As for the meaning of the word "justifiable" in the traditional definition of knowledge above, advocates of scientism would have that understood in quite narrow terms indeed — terms solely derived from philosophical materialism (once again: "a philosophical system which regards matter as the only reality in the world, [and] which undertakes to explain every event in the universe as resulting from the conditions and activity of matter"). So, then, we must ask, which comes first: philosophical materialism or the scientific method? It's a simple question, and one that believers in scientism would often prefer to ignore. If one answers that materialist philosophy is the best foundation for doing science (allegedly the sole basis of legitimate knowledge), then one honestly should confess as well that this is nothing more than a dogmatic assertion, a belief that can't itself be demonstrated through methods of empirical science. If one says, however, that the scientific method is the foundation of philosophical materialism . . . well, frankly, no thinking person could accept this because, once again, nothing of the sort could ever be demonstrated solely by using the scientific method. The statement presumes an ideal, not a concrete fact. And, further, no matter what an advocate of scientism may assert, good science can be done, and has been done, by those who do not believe in philosophical materialism. Good science proves only the truth of science's inestimable value. But there it stops. It can't tell us about things outside its purview. It can't teach us about morality or explain the truth of a poem or a myth or convincingly reveal "the way of a man with a maid." It has nothing whatsoever to tell us about the existence or non-existence of God. Nothing, zip, period. A dogmatic advocate of scientism will insist that it does, but he's talking through his hat.

And there's the difficulty for the modern age: one form of dogmatism is giving place to another form of dogmatism. Even if scientism might be said to have firmer ground for acceptance than religion (which is doubtful), it still hasn't got what it takes to escape the considered opinion of many sound and even brilliant minds that it is just another narrow-minded, inflexible version of fundamentalism. Its most zealous adherents won't acknowledge that they could, just possibly, even remotely, be wrong about their closed system of belief. Such zeal, such fanaticism, regarding science should worry us. Certainly it can be said that we enjoy countless daily benefits from the work of scientists, but there are also many grave evils that science has created for us. Monstrous weapons, deadly viruses, horrific industrial pollution, contaminated and dubiously modified foodstuffs, incompetently manufactured pharmaceuticals — and the list could go on. In the face of science's grand failures, atheistic scientism looks little better than Faustian hubris and moral blindness. But, that evident fact notwithstanding, it is fast becoming the fashionable dogmatism of the post-Christendom world.

One push of scientism in particular should give us cause for trepidation, and that is in the field of neuroscience. Many neuroscientists are reductionists and materialists of the first order, and ideologues to boot. Faith, will, consciousness, aesthetics, and more are for them all reducible to the brain and its functions. The self and human will are considered illusions created by the gray matter in our skulls. Whether or not the brain produces what we call the mind or consciousness has not, in fact, been proved one way or the other. But, as materialists, neuroscientists of a scientistic stripe assume that it must and dogmatically assert that it does. They may be right, or they may be wrong; either way, though, consciousness cannot be reduced to a simple brain function — the mind is altogether more subtle and (dare I say it?) more "miraculous" than that. And, just to assume for the moment that these scientists are wrong about the nature of the mind's relationship to the brain (the mind being in some mysterious way we cannot conceive the operator and the brain that which is being operated), then, in sheer ignorance, to reduce consciousness to the workings of the brain might even be akin to "explaining" radio signals by examining a radio receiver or the Internet by referring to the inner components of a computer.

We are being told that it is only a matter of time before we will be able — with the use of functional magnetic resonance imaging (fMRI) — to read all our desires, motives, sexual wants, and social behaviors with acute accuracy. Then, some are trumpeting, we will have cures for the many things that ail humanity. Another term for this, of course, is social engineering — and presumably the ones who will, with political support, do the manipulating would be the folks in lab coats. As with Fascist and Soviet ideologies of the past, the brave new world envisioned by scientistic neuroscientists is one stripped of humanity as it is, to be replaced by a version of their own invention and tinkering. Visions of *One Flew Over the Cuckoo's Nest* come to mind, with "kindly" neuroscientistic Nurse Ratcheds overseeing our society's future mental hygiene.

Since, in the imagination of advocates of scientism, all questions of meaning and purpose have already been answered by evolutionary science, neuroscience, etcetera, and rendered meaningless and purposeless by the hard philosophy of materialism, then man is finally free to reinvent man. Of course, in reality, they have answered no question. Materialism is only a paltry and arid philosophy, and scientism — like any other form of totalitarian thinking — is at best delusional and at worst potentially horrific.

THE ETHICS OF WARFARE

Christendom has also receded from its old role as guide and arbiter in other matters of morality. Consider conflict and war.

Whereas Jesus stood firmly opposed to violence in all forms, with Christendom came the theory of "just war." Although not perfectly in accord with the principles of the kingdom of God, the "just war theory" nonetheless had been the church's way of delimiting the methods, means, and even the permitted times and seasons of warfare. The gracious rules of medieval chivalry, for example, grew from the benign influence of Christianity working on the warlike tendencies of European cultures and tribes. To make war on non-combatants, to mention just one prohibition for a "just war," was considered a seriously evil crime to commit. There was no idea in those ages of dismissing butchery and rapaciousness as "collateral damage." Potential violence was thereby curbed and discouraged, if not blotted out. As the modern age developed from the Renaissance on, however, Christendom's way of regulated war was let go bit by bit. By the era of the American Civil War, firing missiles into civilian populations — as Sherman did, for instance, throughout the Southern states in his "march to the sea" — was considered a satisfactory method of conducting war. By the twentieth century, there could in fact no longer be any legitimate way of waging war under the terms of Christendom's "just war theory"; but by no means did that make war obsolete for those nations that claimed the heritage of Christendom, as we too well know.

SEXUALITY, PORNOGRAPHY, ABORTION

Christendom's slippage from moral authority can be seen, of course, in many other facets of modern life. Sexuality is an obvious area where this is undeniably the case. The abortion industry is one manifestation of our culture's sexual turpitude. Another example here is pornography. It is one of America's most lucrative industries, and it has gone mainstream in the last few decades and become very nearly ubiquitous. The damaging impact on family life, relationships, healthy interaction between the sexes in every walk of life, on women's dignity especially (but also on that of children and men), the confusions over "sexual identity" (a bizarre term, if ever there was one), the spread of sexually transmitted diseases, and so on, needs no demonstration — it's in the news daily with every report of assault, exploitation, sexual abuse of all ages (and even species), serial murders, and so forth. Pornography is more often than not at the root of all these things, if not as the sole stimulus, then certainly as a crucial contributing factor. When an institution like the Roman Catholic Church, formerly a trusted voice in the world for morality and justice, discovers that it has had a serious problem with pedophiles and their protectors within its ranks of clergy on an unprecedented scale, and has had to undergo the blowback of that shameful revelation, the poisons of a pornographic age can be seen to have contaminated every area of Christendom to an alarming extent. Nor can the minority of Americans striving for a more decent and noble society expect their government to do much about this deluge. With ample mendacity and the willful twisting of meanings long accepted, pornography has become protected as a form of "free speech." The reason for this is clear. In a nation which celebrates *laissez-faire* capitalist greed, one need only realize that pornography rakes in quite a lot of income for its employees and lots of revenue in taxes. Congressional representatives always know where their bread is buttered.

GREED AND STATISM

And that brings up another symptom of Christendom's slippage: the glorification of unchecked greed and consumption. . . . But this is enough. The chief point has been sufficiently made.

So, allow me to return to just one final characteristic of our post-Christendom, which I mentioned in the Introduction, and that is *the latest version of empire-building in the world today*: the growth of American *statism*. It is a challenge for both American Christians, whose military speaks quite explicitly of a new age of *Pax Americana* — a blatant echoing of the *Pax Romana* — and for all those nations of the world affected by American expansionism. What is meant here, of course, is the intrusion on the world stage of a dominant America, rooted in a clearly defined ideology of supremacy, and a peace forced upon the world by American might. With the collapse of the Soviet Union, America now is the world's greatest secular power.

At the time of this writing, I heard a sound bite from a presidential campaign speech by Mitt Romney, in which he said something we've all heard many times in many forms from many American politicians: "I will insist on a military so powerful no one would ever think of challenging it." There, in so many words, is the velvet-covered monkey wrench of American empire, the not-so-subtle threat of this epoch's current superpower. That there is a large contingent in the U.S. military of committed (and hawkish) Christian fundamentalists is, of course, a fact that has been noted with alarm, especially by Mikey Weinstein and his "Military Religious Freedom Foundation." But Weinstein's understandable alarm is coupled with an Americanism that is, in essence, itself antithetical to authentic Christianity. The quote of Weinstein's that one finds at the head of his organization's Web site should be a profound discouragement to any Christian who, seeking to follow the way of Jesus, is also considering joining the armed forces of the American empire today: "When one proudly dons a U.S. Military uniform, there is only one religious symbol: the American flag. There is only one religious scripture: the American Constitution. Finally, there is

only one religious faith: American patriotism." (See http://www
.militaryreligiousfreedom.org.)

Let's be completely honest about the American agenda.
When the United States (with its NATO allies) goes to war today
in other people's countries, it does so primarily to protect its eco-
nomic interests, although it usually thinly conceals this motive
behind some form of interventionist course of action or claims
that this action is necessary (ludicrously enough) to "protect our
freedoms." That is simple fact, and those who dispute it are up
against a wealth of evidence to the contrary.

My meaning here is this: whatever is left of Christendom in
American empire-building is mostly a matter of rhetoric, if not
propaganda. Those who earnestly believe in such things as America's godly beginnings and its divine purpose in the world (once
called "Manifest Destiny," and now sometimes called "American
exceptionalism") are accepting a religious perspective. Religious
it may be, but it emphatically isn't the kingdom of God as Jesus
proclaimed it that they affirm; their pious patriotism is instead
the waning vision of old Christendom. It is the last dollop of that
potent mix of belief in divine predestination working through
history with the goals of a this-worldly empire bent on conquest,
as I put it above. We may see it elsewhere too — in post–USSR
Russia, for instance, where the old specter of Byzantine Christendom has been waxing a bit more brightly of late; but, in America,
we are witnessing the last few expiring gasps of Christendom.

In its place comes — what?

More importantly, in its place comes *what* for those following
Jesus and seeking his kingdom in a post-Christendom world?

TWO

SAYING YES TO DOGMA,
AND NO TO DOGMATISM

The interest of Christianity, what it wants, is — true Christians.

Søren Kierkegaard, *Attack upon "Christendom,"* 1854-1855

I.

Kierkegaard's statement above forces the question — just as he would have wished it — "What makes a *true* Christian?" A short answer, one which has satisfied Christendom for the better part of two thousand years, is *right belief.* The word for adherence to right belief is *orthodoxy* — meaning, literally, "right glory," in the sense of "glorifying" ("praising") God through the confession of correct doctrine. To be orthodox, one is expected to affirm certain dogmas, which are deemed foundational and indispensable. One might hold any number of doctrines that are open to dispute; but dogmas are not disputable and thus are essential to what it means to confess the Christian faith.

Ideally, then, one might think, sensibly enough, that dogmas would be few in number — clear, unperplexing, and plainly stated beliefs. Indeed, the kind of assertions we find in, say, the ancient Apostles' Creed:

I believe in God, the Father almighty,
creator of heaven and earth.
I believe in Jesus Christ, his only Son, our Lord,
who was conceived by the Holy Spirit,
born of the Virgin Mary,
suffered under Pontius Pilate,
was crucified, died, and was buried;
he descended to the place of the dead [Latin, *ad ínferos*].
On the third day he rose again;
he ascended into heaven,
he is seated at the right hand of the Father,
and he will come to judge the living and the dead.
I believe in the Holy Spirit,
the holy catholic Church,
the communion of saints,
the forgiveness of sins,
the resurrection of the body,
and the life everlasting.
Amen.

The early church, before the time of Constantine, used this and other similar creedal statements as expressions of its *regula fidei,* or "rule of faith" (also called the *analogia fidei* — "analogy of faith"; or, by Irenaeus of Lyons, the *kanon tis alethia* — "canon of truth"). These were statements of dogma, which is to say that they were indispensable and foundational orthodox concepts rendered in short, pithy lines, easily digested and memorized.

And it is truly worth emphasizing just how spare the Apostles' Creed is, how economical, and how much space is left for thought about each one of its assertions. It isn't complicated, nor is it unintelligent. It strikes just the right note, neither too high nor too low. For example, take the first line: "I believe in God, the

Father almighty, creator of heaven and earth." Here we have God as Jesus presented him: a "Father" — that is to say, a parental householder who cares for his children. He's not a distant and uncaring deity. Furthermore, in contradistinction to those early Gnostic sects that denied that the material creation is good or that the Father created it, God is here affirmed to be the creator — and therefore, by implication, the creation is presented as good also. This is, again, a point of belief which is in perfect conformity with the teachings of Jesus, who described his Father as fashioning and working through nature. It's a simple statement, but a fundamental and necessary one for the follower of Christ. It can't be proven in a way that would satisfy either an ancient Gnostic (who insisted darkly that the material order is a sham) or a modern materialist scientist (who insists just as darkly that the material order is all there is). But it makes all the difference in (and of) the world for the follower of Christ, who insists that the material order has a meaning and a purpose we cannot fathom without reference to God as revealed by Jesus. In other words, it's a *dogma* in the purest and best sense — foundational, basic, vital, and necessary. Not every one of the statements in the creed is as clear in meaning as this one, but they are all recognizably foundational concepts deriving from Jesus and his immediate followers. Part of the beauty of their simplicity is, at least to my mind, their open-endedness; they leave room for reflection and discussion. Each line is short enough to provide definition and set bounds, but large enough to allow for spiritual exploration and even creativity. It is a "system," but not a stifling one.

Before the age of Christendom, the church sought to give shape and form to its beliefs through such creeds. At the same time, the biblical canon was taking shape as well (which will be the subject of the following chapter), and the structure of a pastoral authority that could claim authentic descent from the apostles was also evolving. These three developments — orthodox creeds, biblical canon, and credentialed pastoral oversight — grew up together, beginning in the late first century, and they existed solely to define and delineate the proper contours of the heritage of Christianity's first generation over against those who were seen to be misrepresenting it. The guiding idea, as the first generation of leaders was passing away, was to keep disciples as close to the original deposit as possible.

The New Testament reveals a church that was already, before the year 100, faced with divisions and arguments over aspects of the faith. The first dilemma faced by the church, as Gentile converts flooded into it, was the Christian movement's increasingly strained relationship to its parent religion, Judaism. Later troubles came from within as various "Gnostic" interpretations of the faith, Gentile and cosmopolitan in origin, were introduced. We see tensions between (Jewish and Gentile) followers of Jesus in Judea and elsewhere and (other) Jews as early as the earliest writing in the New Testament. This was Paul's First Letter to the Thessalonians, and it was most likely written a little more than two decades after Jesus' ministry, in 52. We find, too, that there was pronounced unrest within the churches four decades or so later, as is evident from even the most cursory look through some of the last epistles of the canon — 2 Peter, Jude, and the Johannine letters. In other words, there were controversies from the very start, some Jewish in origin and many more that were Gentile. So it is the case that when we refer to *dogma* in that period — a word that means "to seem" or an "opinion" — we are talking about something intended to correct a misleading notion or doctrine within the context of a controversy. It's a word that refers to the sort of teaching that keeps us on the right road, preventing us from veering to the right or to the left and landing in a ditch or at a dead end: a sort of road marker.

The root for the word *dogma* — *dokeo* — is actually used regarding the decision at the apostolic council in Jerusalem in Acts 15:28. It is my belief that here we find the best and most pristine idea of what dogma is and should be among Christ's followers. Questions had arisen in the early church regarding the grounds for fellowship between Jewish and Gentile Christians: Did male Gentile converts need to be circumcised, and what was needed for them all to share in common meals together in a "kosher" fashion (and, presumably, in communion)? The council's "dogma" was, in this instance, *pragmatic;* that is to say, it dealt with *practices* within the conduct of fellowship, seeking to hold the fellowship together: "For it has seemed [past tense of *dokeo* — *edoxen*] good to the Holy Spirit and to us to lay upon you no greater burden than these necessary things. . . ."

Let's pause there a moment and note three aspects of that decision. *First,* the pronouncement was for the sake of maintaining unity. It sought to prevent division and hold the community together. *Second,* the council members went to some length to add no burden to those receiving their decision — neither intellectual nor moral burdens. The apostles put no unnecessary strains on either Jewish or Gentile believers (and, as we know from the sources available to us, these two groups continued to have marked differences in their respective religious observances for many years to come). *Third,* the council members sought to maintain unity, but without sacrificing "necessary things" or "essentials." In other words, there are essentials in belief and practice that can't be set aside. There are things that are legitimately and necessarily *dogmatic.* (In this case, these had to do with basic food regulations and proscribed forms of sexual practice.)

All three of these aspects are important if we would like to know what ideally constitutes a true dogma. Maintaining unity among diverse believers, not laying unnecessary burdens in faith and practice on people (see Matt. 23:4), and adhering to a few doctrinal essentials — if this example from the earliest age of Christianity had guided all future exercises in defining dogma in the history of the church, what a strikingly different history we might have enjoyed!

It could be noted here that the "dogma" of Acts 15 is entirely a matter of pragmatism and not belief, and that what the church later meant by "dogma" was the definition of an article of conceptual belief (as in "I believe in God, the Father almighty" above). That's a fair point, and I concur with it. Still, we should note that all affirmations of orthodoxy imply orthopraxy — which is to say that "right glory" (theology) implies "right practice" or "right behavior." Orthodox belief and orthopractic morality are inextricably entwined in Christianity. The two are never seen in separate compartments in the New Testament, for example. Every epistle, for instance, matches doctrinal premises with explicit instructions on how to live rightly. Further, if we say in the creed above that "God, the Father almighty," is the "creator of heaven and earth," the ethical implication of that dogmatic assertion is that we should take proper care of God's creation. Likewise, if we profess dogmatically that Christ gave his life for all human beings, then we ethically infer that all are loved by him and not to be despised. And, if we say dogmatically that we believe "in the holy catholic Church" and "the communion of saints," as stated in the Apostles' Creed, we see how the dogmatic decisions of Acts 15 — decreed in order to maintain unity — were just as doctrinal in their basis as they were practical in result, since the apostles were dedicated to keeping the church in communion.

Now, permit me to leap forward across the centuries, long past Constantine and the advent of Christendom, to the year 1854, and to the proclamation of another dogma, this time in the Roman Catholic Church, which is the largest representative body of post-Constantinian Christendom on earth. The dogma I want to consider here, very briefly, is that of the "Immaculate Conception of the Blessed Virgin Mary." Theologians had been debating the doctrine for centuries, and it had met with all the rigors of medieval Scholastic hairsplitting. The church had long asserted that Mary was sinless throughout her life. However, since Augustine's theology had become orthodoxy in the West (though never in the East), the question was not whether or not Mary had ever actually committed a sin (the church, East and West, said emphatically that she had not), but whether or not she had, with the rest of humanity, inherited "original sin." (Stick with me here, bumpy though the ride will be.) By "original sin," the church meant the original sin *of Adam himself* which infects every human being born into the world, because all humanity derives from Adam.

The East, in contrast, had no doctrine of original sin. We all inherit mortality, according to Eastern Christianity, *but not the guilt of Adam's sin.* That's strictly a Western idea, based on a faulty Latin translation of a single Greek New Testament text (Rom. 5:12), which I simply note here without further ado. When the church in the East said that Mary was sinless, they meant only that she had never committed a sin actively (which Eastern Christians also said about other biblical figures such as Jeremiah the prophet and John the Baptist). It's not my concern here to remark upon the historicity of Adam, except to say that the story of the Fall should be read in a "spiritual sense" and not literally, and that its power lies in what it says about the fallibility of human beings. But, in the West, which had adopted as dogma the theory of Augustine (354-430) that all human beings were born guilty of Adam's sin and were thereby born damned, and only rescued from hell through baptism (the washing away of original sin), the question in the case of Mary's alleged sinlessness was whether or not she had contracted original sin. If Mary had been conceived with Adam's original sin, the church could not claim — as it had long claimed — that she was *sinless*. As I said, this was a conundrum that had exercised Latin theological minds for centuries.

We may note here, as well, that the Augustinian interpretation of the early chapters of Genesis forces upon us a *heightened biblical literalism*. The Western interpretation of the Genesis account, which historicized it to a degree that couldn't help but stretch credulity as the sciences grew, came at the expense of a potentially more flexible (and spiritually nourishing) reading of that story, and it has continued to be a problem for Catholic and Protestant "orthodox" theologians ever since.

At any rate, if the underpinning theology of the "Immaculate Conception of Mary" confuses you, or leaves you asking "So what?," you are perhaps catching a glimpse of the serious fact that something drastic has changed between the attitude about dogma we see in the Apostles' Creed or the council of Jerusalem in Acts 15, and that which underlies the pronouncement of the Marian dogma of 1854. I won't go into any more detail about it; I'll simply say that the pope declared in the latter decision that Mary was "conceived without taint of original sin" — she was "immaculately" ("sinlessly") conceived. The atonement wrought by Christ, through his cross and resurrection, was said to work "retroactively" in the case of his mother.

We doubtless have a quandary here if we accept (as the early church seems to have done) that a dogmatic belief has pragmatic implications. To put the question candidly, with the dogma of the Immaculate Conception of Mary, what precisely are we to derive from this doctrine that is necessary for our Christian life? What good does believing it do us? And, to ask the question in reverse, what harm does it do, since it obliges us to accept as its theoretical root a historicized and literal reading, against all reason, of a fabulous biblical text best left to spiritual interpretation? Given its basis in what was from the outset a novel interpretation of the Fall (Augustine's strange and hitherto unknown fifth-century doctrine of Adam's original sin, passed down to all humanity and damning it), and despite its being a debating point for centuries in the West, this very late dogma (1854!) looks suspiciously like a mythological concept that has been so historicized, Scholasticized, debated, and finally defined that whatever spiritual benefit might at one time have been associated with a mystical notion of Mary's sinlessness, if any can be ascertained, has long since receded from view. It has become an article to be affirmed among a long list of articles. More than that, it is so abstruse an article that even many Roman Catholics have difficulty understanding it or its rationale, often confusing it with the virginal conception of Jesus Christ. Even more troubling still, it is one more dogma (among others) that further divides West from East, and Catholic from Protestant, putting yet another unnecessary stumbling block in the path of Christian unity.

In Acts 15, as noted above, we saw these three elements as implicit to the dogma the council of Jerusalem promoted: maintenance of unity among believers, no laying down of unnecessary burdens in faith and practice on disciples, and adherence to a few doctrinal essentials. We saw that the Apostles' Creed and the early church's *regula fidei* kept within those same bounds, despite the divisiveness that threatened Christianity from its inception. With Christendom, however, we see the beginnings of a different mood within the imperially endorsed religion. The emperor Constantine himself wanted a single religion with a single creed, not a religion with a range of doctrinal differences. By the early fourth century, divisions among Christians had become more philosophically speculative in nature. Did Jesus have one or two natures? Was there a time when he had not existed, or had he existed from all eternity? In what sense was he divine? *Was* he divine? And so forth. The difficulties were numerous, and the emperor — who saw himself as the guardian of both the empire and its faith — wanted the church's bishops to sort them out. In 325 he summoned the bishops of the church to the city of Nicaea to hold a council there, and from that council came the first version of what in time would be called the Nicene (or Nicene-Constantinopolitan) Creed.

My intention here is not to go into the history of the church's councils and creeds. There are many books that explore that history thoroughly and well already. I simply wish to note that the Nicene Creed — which is unquestionably a magnificent statement of Christian belief — differs markedly from the Apostles' Creed in its elaboration of theological concepts. In its favor, it is no more theoretically rich or challenging in nature than is, say, the Gospel of John or the epistles of Paul, and it offers us much for reflection. It still allows a great deal of flexibility and possesses both subtlety and poetic vigor. On a less positive note, the council of Nicaea, with its anathemas and its association with imperial power, sets the stage for Christendom's movement from dogmas as road markers in the service of maintaining both doctrinal and practical unity, to dogmas as increasingly abstruse and abusive.[1] The move is from dogma to *dogmatism,* which Hans Küng has said "consists of the exaggeration, isolation, and absolutization of dogma." He continues, "The valuable teaching contained in dogma is transformed into doctrinalism and its binding nature degenerates into juridicism. The partial becomes the particularist, the authoritative the authoritarian, the intellectual the ratio-

---

1. A popular, readable, and somewhat unnerving account of this age and its early councils, as well as the intrigues and violence associated with it, is *When Jesus Became God: The Struggle to Define Christianity during the Last Days of Rome,* by Richard E. Rubenstein (New York: Harcourt, 1999).

nalist, and the trend to formulation and objectification finally leads to a formalism, objectivism, and positivism that crush the truth with truths."[2]

With dogmatism and its legacy we are a far cry from the first-century concern for allowing doctrinal and practical leeway, with emphasis laid only upon those recognizably foundational statements that all followers of Jesus should be able to affirm in their own way. Paul's wise counsel to the church in Rome, made up of Jewish and Gentile believers with a variety of customs, that their personal practice of "the faith that you [singular] have [should be kept] between yourself and God" (Rom. 14:22; but see the entire chapter), has been forgotten. With Christendom's flourishing dogmatism comes an increasing foliation of abstractions and fine points which must be affirmed on pain of damnation. Orthodoxy degenerates into doctrinal obsession, and human lives are held in a balance as a real result. Notoriously, the sixth-century Latin (and theologically Augustinian) *Quicunque vult* — the mis-named "Athanasian Creed" — opens its profession of faith by condemning "everlastingly" all who do not profess it with all the rigorous precision the text requires. Its multitude of abstract assertions regarding the Trinity and the two natures of Christ are a masterpiece of obsessive fine-tuning mixed with threat. It is difficult for anyone acquainted with the church's history not to recall, when reading this belligerent exercise in dogmatism, that many human beings — those "for whom Christ died" (Rom. 14:15) — were in fact tortured and killed for failing to acknowledge just such doctrinal obscurities. Perhaps more strikingly, it might be noted that there is a total absence in this text of anything deriving from Jesus himself, either in word or in spirit.

2. Hans Küng, *Infallible?: An Unresolved Enquiry* (New York: Continuum, 1994), pp. 141-42.

The cure for dogmatism is *pragmatism*. Dogma certainly has legitimacy in the future of Christianity, but not dogmatism; and what can restore dogma to its proper dimensions and purpose is a restoration of its true value as seen *in practice*. Will it, in other words, maintain unity among believers (and not be a source of division), refrain from laying down unnecessary burdens in faith and practice on disciples (instead of piling up abstruse and perplexing articles of belief which are, in the final analysis, both practically and theoretically meaningless), and adhere only to a few doctrinal essentials (rather than a superfluity of doctrinal abstractions)? To put it another way, can there be dogma with discipline — the discipline of restraint and pragmatic pastoral sensitivity?

II.

Thomas Aquinas (1225-1274), the greatest of the medieval Scholastic theologians, author of the enormous *Summa Theologica* and the *Summa contra Gentiles,* refuter of heresies and conflater of revelation and reason, had an experience near the end of his life which overwhelmed him and brought his amazing productivity to a permanent halt. While saying Mass one morning in Naples, he heard something like thunder from above. It so jolted and altered him that he never completed the *Summa*. When pressed to continue work on it, he claimed that he could not. "Everything I have written," he reportedly said, "seems as worthless as straw." This shock of realization, in the wake of a mystical experience, had moved him to re-evaluate the value of his former Scholastic efforts. His conclusion was that they had been weighed in the balance of his sudden numinous insight and found wanting.

Thomas apparently had become inwardly convicted at this late juncture in his life that he really could not construct a comprehensive intellectual system which adequately defined ultimate verities, no matter how well-reasoned, ornate, beautiful, or intricate he made it. Thomas had always been a notably humble man as well as a brilliant one. It might be said of him too, with some carefulness, that he had perhaps become a sort of philosophical Pragmatist at the end, ironically because he had personally experienced something transcendent in nature (and one doesn't typically think of mysticism and Pragmatism coming together; although — as we will see — William James did). Thomas had been unexpectedly made aware of something so vast in scope that his theological system now appeared to him, in comparison, to be dry, brittle stuff. Using philosophical terminology of a much later age, this is a primary insight of what goes by the name of Pragmatism.

Historically, Pragmatism is a distinctively Anglo-American philosophical school, having to do with ideas that "work" in contrast to those that don't, or at least are so disconnected from real life that they don't much matter. As schools of philosophy go, it's an eminently sensible one. Pragmatism is associated with such distinguished names in the history of American thought as Charles Sanders Pierce (1839-1914; his surname is pronounced "purse"; and he is alleged to have been Pragmatism's originator through an article published in 1878), Josiah Royce (1855-1916), John Dewey (1859-1952), and — most eccentrically — George Santayana (1863-1952). Today one associates it with the names of Richard Rorty and Hilary Putnam. Arguably, though, it was William James (1842-1910) who made it genuinely winsome and persuasive as a philosophy, especially in the 1906-1907 series of lectures he presented both at the Lowell Institute in Boston and at Columbia University in Manhattan, and later published as the small book *Pragmatism*. The latter was not everywhere well-received at the time, but it nonetheless has exercised a lasting influence ever since.

As James explained, the word "pragmatism" comes from the Greek for "action" *(pragma),* and is related to other English words such as "practice" and "practical." As already noted, Pragmatism is in fact concerned with practicalities: What, say, are the *practical* results of believing *this* as opposed to believing *that?* What are the *real consequences* if I hold such-and-such to be *true* or to possess *meaning?*

Its boldest claim, perhaps, has to do with the nature of truth (and this will start to lead us back in the direction of our discussion of dogma): in the words of William James, *"The true is the name of whatever proves itself to be good in the way of belief, and good, too, for definite, assignable reasons."*[3] The position James takes here is that truth, whatever it may be in itself, can only be *partially* knowable to us. In its entirety or absoluteness, it is unknowable. In other words, there is always more truth to be apprehended, and even our capacity for truth is limited by our particular perceptions of things (for instance, creatures different from ourselves can *perceive* the *same* truth quite differently than we are able to). Pragmatism is, as I've said, a position of humility and open-mindedness before the truth we can never fully embrace; and this is the case for the simple reason that human beings can know only a mere fragment of reality, one that fits the small abilities and meager perspectives of a very tiny creature in an incalculably vast universe. (When we look back at one of our subjects in the first chapter, we can see that the greatest fault of scientism is its inability to acknowledge this undeniable

3. William James, *Pragmatism,* Library of America edition (New York: The Library of America, 1987), p. 520; italics in the original.

fact adequately, choosing rather to believe that human science can someday achieve a sort of human omniscience.) Not only is this essentially a "pragmatic" position vis-à-vis reality; it's also — when deeply felt by an individual in a moment of special awareness — profoundly mystical in nature. This kind of special awareness is what, I suspect, silenced the (misnamed) *Summa* of Thomas Aquinas.

We human beings are really only bits of a "system" we did not create, do not govern, and — except to the most infinitesimal and negligible degree imaginable — can never hope to manipulate or genuinely influence. We are very probably not even the universe's cleverest systematizers or knowers of truth. We do not stand outside the immeasurable box of creation, and therefore we can never actually be objective about it. All our perceptions and cogitations are relative to our extremely limited capacities. We do not have "the mind of God," whether we are theologians or physicists, and certainly never will acquire such exalted intelligence before our earthly existence ends. The notion that we could ever formulate a "unified theory of everything" is an absurdity almost childish in its naïveté. James put it this way in a memorable passage:

> I firmly disbelieve, myself, that our human experience is the highest form of experience extant in the universe. I believe rather that we stand in much the same relation to the whole of the universe as our canine and feline pets do to the whole of human life. They inhabit our drawing-rooms and libraries. They take part in scenes of whose significance they have no inkling. They are merely tangent to curves of history the beginnings and ends and forms of which pass wholly beyond their ken. So we are tangent to the wider life of things.[4]

4. James, *Pragmatism*, p. 619.

Truth, as the italicized definition from William James above makes clear, is related to *belief* (i.e., "faith" or "trust"), and also to *proof* — the end result — of a belief's practical *goodness*. "Goodness" in what sense, we may ask? James tells us: Goodness *"in the sense of being good for so much."*[5] That is to say, truth is measurable by a standard of goodness; it is found in what is weighed and proved by experience to be beneficial for us, in ways we can understand according to our limited capacities for moral discernment.

This not a case for moral relativism, as it might come across, nor is it an apology for social experimentation. Pragmatists like James might speak of our "creating truth," but only in the sense that truth is alive when it is put into action in concrete circumstances, not while it remains an unpracticed theory. One can "create" falsehood and evil as well, it should be added; actions do not become "true" simply because they have been willed into actuality, much less are they "good" thereby. Truth is made real in goodness concretely lived, existentially, not in sheer speculation about high ideals or universal ideas, as useful as these may be in forming our thinking.

James and the early Pragmatists still believed that a moral order existed in the universe and that it could be seen in the effects of how men and women actually conducted their lives. They possessed an optimism that has since been eroded by two world wars and other monstrous events. Most of them still believed, however tenuously or curiously defined, in God. For his part, James was quite unequivocal about the matter. (However, had James and the rest lived through that ugliest, most degrading, and most atheistic of centuries — the twentieth — they might, paradoxically, have embraced Pragmatism all the more, having

5. James, *Pragmatism*, p. 519; italics in the original.

before them ample evidence of the concrete evils that evil beliefs spawn.)

Pragmatism, then, looks to end results; it evaluates causes by their effects, and not the other way around. "No particular results then, so far, but only an attitude of orientation," writes James, "is what the pragmatic method means. *The attitude of looking away from first things, principles, 'categories,' supposed necessities; and of looking towards last things, fruits, consequences, facts.*"[6] "Fruits, not roots," is an old Pragmatist sentiment, and it is certainly an even older Christian one. Obviously roots are vital things for a fruit-bearing tree, but it is the quality of the fruit we most look for from it. When Jesus cursed the fig tree in the strange, parabolic action recounted in Mark 11, this was the very point he was making.

And, indeed, Pragmatism is an orientation of focus that we can easily recognize as congruent with all biblical thought. Greek philosophers might have looked above and beyond to motion-lessness, changelessness, and eternal ideas; but the Bible looks ahead to transformation and dynamic — indeed, cataclysmic — renewal. The Bible is less concerned with origins than with goals (although it obviously doesn't ignore origins!); it sees history as one great movement into the future — a tiny seed increasing invisibly to gigantic proportions over time, a bit of leaven leavening a whole batch of bread, a field sown with wheat and also tares awaiting the threshing, a catch of edible and inedible fish yet to be separated, a final judgment, a whole creation groaning in travail for the manifestation of the children of God, the final resurrection. . . .

The New Testament is always looking ahead to *goals,* both personal and cosmic in scope. Jesus exhibits this focus repeat-

6. James, *Pragmatism,* p. 510; italics in the original.

edly. Here I choose but one of his sayings from a multitude of possible examples: "Every sound tree bears good fruit, but the bad tree bears evil fruit. A sound tree cannot bear evil fruit, nor can a bad tree bear good fruit. Every tree that does not bear good fruit is cut down and thrown into the fire. Thus you will know them by their fruits" (Matt. 7:17-20). The apostle Paul reveals the same attention to goals on almost every page of his epistles, as here, for instance, where he speaks of the personal demands of righteousness: "Forgetting what lies behind and straining forward to what lies ahead, I press on toward the goal for the prize of the upward call of God in Christ Jesus. . . . Only let us hold true to what we have attained" (Phil. 3:13b-14, 16).

The thrust is forward, and *results* are what reveal the truth — the soundness — of a belief; and this is so whether we refer to the belief of an individual, a community, or the world. It isn't anachronistic to say that it is the Pragmatist mind we hear voiced in the Letter of James, where, possibly addressing the speculative theologians of his own day, the author writes, "You believe that God is one; you do well. Even the demons believe — and shudder" (James 2:19). In that terse statement we have a pragmatic mind expressing its disdain for the ineffectually speculative: even demons can be fine theologians in the latter sense. When the same writer goes on to say that "faith without works is dead," the idea is not far removed from the Pragmatists' claim that our actions "create" the truth we profess (James 2:20, KJV).

Following a brilliant passage in *The Varieties of Religious Experience* in which William James quotes extensively from John Henry Cardinal Newman (1801-1890) on the transcendent attributes of God, he points out both the scintillating beauty of Newman's prose and — where human action based on such dogmatic assertions is concerned — the impracticality of the concepts amassed there. As the following passage makes clear, James has no intention of impugning Newman or questioning his greatness as a theologian and thinker. Nevertheless, writes James,

> What I have given will serve as a specimen of the orthodox philosophical theology of both Catholics and Protestants. Newman, filled with enthusiasm at God's list of perfections, continues the passage which I began to quote to you by a couple of pages of a rhetoric so magnificent that I can hardly refrain from adding them in spite of the inroad they would make upon our time. He first enumerates God's attributes sonorously, then celebrates his ownership of everything in earth and Heaven, and the dependence of all that happens upon his permissive will. He gives us scholastic philosophy "touched with emotion," and every philosophy should be touched with emotion to be rightly understood. Emotionally, then, dogmatic theology is worth something to minds of the type of Newman's.[7]

But then James continues with this criticism:

> What God has joined together, let no man put asunder. The Continental schools of philosophy have too often overlooked the fact that man's thinking is organically connected to his conduct. It seems to me to be the chief glory of English and Scottish thinkers to have kept the organic connection in view. The guiding principle of British philosophy has in fact been that every difference must *make* a difference, every theoretical difference somewhere issue in a practical difference, and that the best method of discussing points of theory is to begin by ascertaining what practical difference would result from one alternative or the other being true. What is the par-

---

7. William James, *The Varieties of Religious Experience*, Library of America edition (New York: The Library of America, 1987), pp. 397-98.

ticular truth in question *known as?* In what facts does it result? . . . For what seriousness can possibly remain in debating philosophical propositions that will never make an appreciable difference to us in action? And what would it matter, if all propositions were practically indifferent, which of them we should agree to call true or which false?[8]

James makes the same point elsewhere in an even sharper — perhaps excessively so — passage. Compiling a list of Scholastic definitions, he then evaluates their worth:

> "Deus est Ens, a se, extra et supra omne genus, necessarium, unum, infinite perfectum, simplex, immutabile, immensum, aeternum, intelligens," etc. ["God is being, from itself, above and beyond all kinds, necessary, one, infinitely perfect, simple, unchanging, great, eternal, the principle of thought"] — wherein is such a definition really instructive? It means less than nothing, in its pompous robe of adjectives.[9]

We can disagree vehemently with James on this point, of course. Are these adjectives really "pompous," or are they an attempt to grasp within the limitations of language those mysterious attributes of divinity that have been glimpsed, but also known to be ultimately ungraspable? Such caveats aside, it's not as simple as that James was stubbornly at odds with all speculation about the nature of God, although he found it next to no worth for himself. Rather, once again, his main point is that faith should be related to action, and that all abstract ideas about God (or anything else, for that matter) must be weighed by what

8. James, *The Varieties of Religious Experience,* pp. 398-99.
9. James, *Pragmatism,* p. 539.

they produce in the lives of those who hold them. One can be impressed to the point of entrancement by the lines of deft reasoning one discovers in Aquinas, or captivated by the exquisite prose of Newman, stimulated by the magisterial and the beautiful in both; but just possibly James comes closer than either to the most manifest concerns of the biblical writers in his stress on the pragmatic. In fact, one can comb the Bible exhaustively and find precious little in the way of dogmatic abstractions about the nature of the Godhead — and certainly nothing that sounds very much like either Aquinas or Newman. This is true of the words of Christ, whose revelation of the character of God is paramount for Christians. In fact, there was never a figure more pragmatic in what he taught than Jesus.

This is not to suggest that we don't need theology, in the sense of deep and prayerful reflection on the being and nature of God. But, without a pragmatic ethical focus, theology can degenerate into such cul-de-sacs as dogmatic hairsplitting, scriptural fundamentalism (which is the collapsing of spiritual into literal meaning), superstition (the confusion of faith with irrationality and magical thinking), or the sort of legalistic religion that presses down rather than lifts up the human being. Such things understandably render religious belief ridiculous in the minds of its critics. As the great Rabbi Abraham Heschel (1907-1972) writes (returning us to the subject of dogma),

> Of what avail, then, are opinions, words, dogmas? In the confinement of our study rooms, our knowledge seems to us a pillar of light. But when we stand at the door which opens out to the infinite, we realize that all concepts are but glittering motes that populate a sunbeam. . . . Faith is not the assent to an idea, but the consent to God. . . . In other words, what is expressed and taught as a creed is but the adaptation of the uncommon spirit to the common mind.

Our creed is, like music, a translation of the unutterable into a form of expression. The original is known to God alone.[10]

And elsewhere, Heschel writes,

Teachers of religion have always attempted to raise their insights to the level of utterance, dogma, creed. Yet such utterances must be taken as *indications,* as attempts to convey what cannot be adequately expressed, if they are not to stand in the way of authentic faith.[11]

A dogmatic system will likely grow out of the sincerest efforts of deeply motivated and saintly thinkers. But it is always in danger of degenerating through the loss of its mystical impulse and vitality. The uses of Scholasticism — that blending of Aristotelian logic and creedal affirmations, of which the works of Thomas Aquinas are the premier example — within Western Catholicism (but also later within Protestantism, and even, to a lesser extent and through the influence of the West, within Eastern Orthodoxy) were always spiritually limited. This is illustrated by the crowning, silencing realization of Aquinas before he died. What conceals its limitations is the sophistication of its thought. Slicing the baloney ever thinner may make it appear as if something substantial is being multiplied before our eyes, but the nutrients in fact are decreasing with every slice. Scholasticism — as well as dogmatism — reduces even as it multiplies, slicing and dicing theological details into ever more numerous smaller bits. To change the analogy, dogmatism places more and more fences

10. Rabbi Abraham Joshua Heschel, *Man Is Not Alone: A Philosophy of Religion* (New York: Farrar, Straus & Giroux, 1951), pp. 35, 166, 167.

11. Rabbi Abraham Joshua Heschel, *God in Search of Man: A Philosophy of Judaism* (New York: Farrar, Straus & Giroux, 1955), p. 103; italics mine.

around a core belief, which means increasing confinement for the mind of the believers. There is left little space for the spirit to roam. The spirit may freely blow "where it wills," but less and less can the same be said of "every one who is born of the Spirit" if kept under the restraints of dogmatism or Scholasticism (see John 3:8). In the words, once again, of Abraham Heschel, who in turn quotes F. P. Ramsey (1903-1930), the Cambridge mathematician and philosopher, before adding his own comment, "We must keep in mind that 'the chief danger to philosophy, apart from laziness and woolliness, is *scholasticism,* the essence of which is treating what is vague as if it were precise and trying to fit it into an exact logical category.' Indeed," continues Heschel, "one of the fatal errors of conceptual theology has been the separation of the acts of religious existence from the statements about it."[12]

The value of aligning a Pragmatist approach with Christian dogma and spirituality, in contrast to Scholasticism or dogmatism, might be said to lie in a more satisfying *incarnational perspective* as a result. "The Word became flesh and dwelt among us" is the Gospel of John's way of expressing that, in Jesus of Nazareth, what was formerly intangible and — abstractly — theological grist for the speculative mill came down to earth "full of grace and truth" (John 1:14). In itself the Word *(logos)* is, by definition, a *principle,* invisible in its nature to created eyes, and essentially an abstraction for human thought. So the Word would have remained unless it had become incarnated — literally "enfleshed." In so doing, God became visible in human form and was thus "exegeted" *(exegesato)* — interpreted — for us in the life, works, and words of the historical Jesus (John 1:18). This meant divine action and engagement with human beings in all our material

12. Heschel, *God in Search of Man,* pp. 7-8.

existence. No abstractions here. The Gospel of John can be an occasionally difficult and impenetrable book, and its spirituality is exalted; but it is also earthy, "fleshly," and pragmatic. The implications for our lives are obvious: if the eternal Word became flesh, then the words he spoke and the imitation of the deeds he did should be enfleshed in us, too. We should be careful not to stress the "Word" more than the "flesh" in our theology. Ours is a religion centered on the incarnation of God and everything that that implies: "For I have given you an example, that you also should do as I have done to you. . . . If you know these things, blessed are you if you do them" (John 13:15, 17).

The central revelation of Christianity is belief in the Incarnation. It is a pragmatic belief for us, and everything we hold as important for the practice of our faith stems from it. Whether or not we deem ourselves to be Pragmatists in the philosophical or Jamesian sense is immaterial; but to be a Christian is without doubt to be a pragmatist, with Jesus being our model and guide. "Faith without works is dead" (James 2:17, 26, KJV). Faith must be, simply put, pragmatic; and since dogma is an expression of faith that is not "dead," because it is seen in "works," it must be pragmatic as well.

III.

This brings us to a summary of our discussion of dogma. The first point is simply that we must distinguish between *dogma* and *dogmatism*. As we move away more and more from the civilization of Christendom (or, better perhaps, as Christendom recedes from us), and, as strangers and pilgrims, we learn to pitch our tents in the world as it has become, we don't leave behind our dogmas. Dogmas, however, are our signposts on the way each of us must walk. They aren't restraining fences, but point us outward toward our journey, in the direction of wide-open possibilities. As Rabbi Heschel said, they are "indications" of what "cannot be adequately expressed." We need the simple directions Jesus laid out for us, leading us on toward the Father, Son, and Spirit, toward community with one another and life with God, toward a way of living that is real and winsome.

We do not want the dogmatism that grew up as part of the blending of Christianity with the state. It was an abuse of the teachings of Jesus from the outset to imagine that the two could ever be blended seamlessly, a notion wholly at odds with the radical character of the kingdom of God. To the extent that the church accepted or promoted state-sponsored policing and punishment of heretics during the long historical course and assorted forms of Christendom, it was in the wrong. Nor should Christians today seek to reproduce a Constantinian merger of church and state. That day has come and gone, thankfully, and we are strangers and pilgrims once more. Dogmatism (with its many correlate forms of Scholastic systematization) is the tendency to complicate and systematize what never really needed to be complicated or turned into a closed system at all. Dogma should lead to mysticism and morality; but dogmatism has too often led instead to rigidity and the ossification of ideas, and, with it, vicious practices to enforce strict adherence to them. When a dogma is no longer comprehensible to the average follower of Jesus, it is no longer a signpost for his or her life or an indication of anything beyond a definition on paper requiring his or her docile assent.

The second point, and related to the first, is that — taking Acts 15 for our model — dogma should assist Christians in maintaining unity among diverse believers, should never lay unnecessary burdens in faith and practice on disciples of Jesus, and should invite adherence to only a few doctrinal essentials. This is why the Apostles' Creed, for example, which conforms closely to the basic affirmations we find in the Gospels and epistles of the New Testament, is a good statement of dogma; and it is also one of the many reasons why the 1854 definition of the Immaculate Conception of Mary, to take this one example from among many possible ones, is not. Whatever is not recognizable as an original and authoritative teaching, one that is supportive of mutual agreement, a belief easily borne, and clearly essential — taken from Christ and the earliest witnesses — should never be proposed as sound dogma.

And, finally, dogma must be pragmatist in its outlook. If faith — dogma — is dead without works, then the practical fruit of dogma must be seen as proof of its truth. If we believe in the creeds we profess, then our lives must be in alignment with what we affirm. We will find more than enough to live up to in just the three chapters of Matthew's Gospel given to the Sermon on the Mount (Matt. 5–7), not to mention everything else we read in the Gospels and the remainder of the New Testament. If something bears no fruit at all in our Christian lives, it is too barren to be a useful dogma. Belief in God the Father leads to love for all creation, belief in the Son leads to taking Jesus as our exemplar and redeemer, and belief in the Spirit leads to unbreakable communion with our fellow disciples. Dogma leads to changed perspectives, reformed minds, and daring new lives. It points us along a way, and that way is our own life and includes all our experiences, successes and failures both.

If we can hold to dogma as what binds us to God, the creation, other human beings and their full range of needs, and to one another, we will once again — as strangers and pilgrims, with no support from governments and armies and courts and bureaucracies — recover for ourselves the genuine, pragmatic meaning of the dogma we claim.

THREE

SAYING YES TO THE BIBLE,
AND NO TO BIBLICISM

*[The Reformers'] creed has been described as a return
to the Gospel in the spirit of the Koran.*

The Very Rev. W. R. Inge,
The Platonic Tradition in English Religious Thought, 1926

*When interpreted like any other book, by the same rules of
evidence and the same canons of criticism, the Bible will still
remain unlike any other book; its beauty will be freshly seen,
as of a picture which is restored after many ages to its original
state; it will create a new interest and make for itself a new kind
of authority by the life which is in it. It will be a spirit and
not a letter; as it was in the beginning, having an influence like
that of the spoken word, or the book newly found.*

Benjamin Jowett, "On the Interpretation of Scripture," 1860

I.

Whether or not one sees Dean Inge's remark above, regarding
the biblicism of the Protestant Reformers, as a fair appraisal of

their adherence to the doctrine of *sola scriptura,* it does highlight a problem that faces us still, one that should particularly concern Christians as we pitch our pilgrims' tents in the post-Christendom epoch.

That problem is biblical fundamentalism or literalism. It is a mistake to think that "biblicism" (the term I will be using here for biblical fundamentalism) is just a Protestant phenomenon. We find it cropping up here and there throughout Christian history. We can come across it today among Catholics and Orthodox (especially, though not exclusively, in the United States). But the Bible, as Dean Inge was trying to get across, is not supposed to be received by Jews or Christians in the same way that Muslims receive their Koran. The Koran, according to Muslim faith, is simply and literally "the word of God." Thus, every individual word of it is holy — "sacramental," if you will — directly communicated by Allah. A truly faithful Muslim is supposed to learn Arabic, in fact, because the text should really be read as it was given, in the very language in which it was given. That's what Inge meant by the phrase "the spirit of the Koran." And, regarding the fundamentalist strand in Christianity, he was correct to make the comparison and the contrast.

The Bible is not the Koran, and Christians (and Jews) are not Muslims. We do not read the Bible as "a book," for example, but as a collection of books. The Bible is better described as a library. Nor do Christians receive the Bible as the Word of God. That may come as a surprise to some, especially since we are often referred to — wrongly — as "people of the book." But, we are not; and the Word of God is not a book. For us, the Word of God is God himself. We call him, in theological language, "the Son of God" and "the Second Person of the Trinity." We say of him that he "became flesh and dwelt among us." In other words, for Christians, the Word of God is Jesus. He alone "defines" for us fully the character of God; he is the divine writ small, in fleshly, human terms we can see, "read," understand, and follow in our lives. We could not know the divine in its uncreated being, but we could know it in Christ.

When we refer to Scripture as "the word of God," we mean it in a different sense. We mean that, in these books of the Bible, we find a collective testimony to God's existence and interaction with a specific historical people, leading us finally to the one, who, from among that people, we receive as God made man. The Bible is the word of God in the sense that it brings us the word *about* God; but it isn't to be worshiped or venerated as more than a collection of books that give us an outline and a direction for our faith.

It isn't an end in itself, nor is it an authority in itself. It is, like dogma in the last chapter, an indicator and a signpost for what lies beyond its pages. It is "inspired," we believe; that is to say, it is "God-breathed" (2 Tim. 3:16; *theopneustos*), but not dictated word-for-word. One memorable line in 2 Peter puts it like this: "Men moved by [or "carried along by"] the Holy Spirit spoke from God" (1:21). For Scripture to be "God-breathed" means that writers were swept up and borne along, if you will, by a compelling insight, which they expressed in words according to their best abilities and lights. It is, taken as a whole, a grand, epical testimony to a historical community — in fact, *two* historical communities — evolving in an unfolding understanding of God. That evolution is, for the Christian, brought to its fullness with Jesus and the kingdom of God. Christ is the culminating revelation who sheds light on the adequacies and inadequacies of all that came before him in the scriptural record.

One way to describe "biblicism," in contrast to "Bible," is to say that what the former does, in effect, is *flatten* all the biblical books. It makes the rough places plain, certainly — just as plain as a checkerboard. But what happens in the process is that the mountains and valleys of the Bible disappear entirely, the variety of its landscapes goes unperceived, and we are left with the wholly mistaken notion that the Bible is a single book by a single author (God), in which every passage is to be received as of equal value and understood literally. In other words, a Biblicist reading of the Bible could conceivably require one to regard, for example, a passage in Leviticus (let's say one that gives instructions about the high priest's undergarments) as of equal worth as the Sermon on the Mount. Both are, it is believed, "God's word," and therefore must be treated with equal seriousness.

Another difficulty, one frequently raised by friends and foes alike of biblical religion, is how we can line up the violence and bloodshed of the Old Testament, sanctioned supposedly by God himself, with the message of Jesus, who preaches non-violence and love of one's enemies, in the New Testament. A fundamentalist will have many unconvincing ways to hold such things together, never admitting that they simply can't be held together in any rational fashion (and, if pushed, a thoroughgoing fundamentalist may go so far as to deny the value of "human reason" itself in this matter).

Reading these ancient texts literally, a fundamentalist will anachronistically insist on the scientific and historical accuracy of even the most transparently poetic and mythological portions. By any standard, of course, the Bible can be a confusing mixture of genres: fable, legend, history, parables, sayings, prophecies, letters, hymns, and so forth. Shockingly (for some), it includes irreverence (Ecclesiastes, Job), humor (Jonah), and even a dash of eroticism (the Song of Songs). In one unexpected instance, for example, it tells an intentionally hilarious tale about a "wise man" scolded by his talking donkey, right in the middle of a book of law and sacred history (Numbers 22). In another, even more familiar story, all the woes of human history are traced back to another talking beast, the serpent in the Garden; and — at the other end of the Bible — the end of the world is depicted in a dizzying display of apocalyptic images. One thing the Bible most clearly is *not:* it is *not* a single, flat book with a single, flat picture of God.

The Bible, as already said above, is really a collection of many books written and edited over a span of centuries. In Christianity the "canon" is made up of two canons, that of the Old Covenant (the Hebrew Bible) and that of the New. The word "canon" literally means "measuring reed," which is a standard of measurement like a yardstick. In this instance, the *canon* of Scripture provides the dimensions of a revelation as it evolved over time, so that those who carry on its legacy into their own times may do so faithfully. The Bible isn't the entirety of the revelation. It is a standard that sizes up the authenticity of the life and tradition of a community of Christian disciples. The two canons within the overall biblical canon define the identity of the communities that gathered, preserved, edited, and published them in the forms we have received. This is a vital feature to which we shall return. For Christians, both canons taken together provide the essential conceptual context for understanding Jesus and his message. For us, then, Jesus is the key to unlocking the Scriptures, and the Scriptures — in all their variety and occasional contrariness — lead us to a more lucid interpretation of his teachings.

Biblicism will undoubtedly be with us for some time to come. Despite its intellectual bankruptcy, it is tenacious. I don't wish to belabor the issue; it is enough here to reiterate that it doesn't genuinely represent classical Christianity, nor can it ever be a part of the sort of Christianity likely to impress intelligent people in the post-Christendom age. At the risk of sounding elitist (which I don't believe myself to be), it isn't viable or credible for thinking persons. Anyone who insists upon the accuracy of

the "science" in the Bible, for instance (there isn't any), or un-
questioningly takes the Bible's ancient form of historiography
as being as accurate or scrupulous as post-Enlightenment historiography, or fails to acknowledge the variety of literary genres
which can at times show up in even a single book of Scripture, or
who refuses to believe that the Bible includes fable, or contains
noticeable contradictions, is someone who simply misunder-
stands profoundly the nature of the holy book he holds dear.
That person may love Christ and mean well, to be sure; but he is
wrong about the Bible and its place in Christian faith. It may also
be impossible to convince a determined biblical fundamentalist
just how wrong he is. Fundamentalism is a tough nut. Nor is it,
as I said, my wish to argue against such people in these pages.
All I will add, then, before moving on to a larger discussion of
biblical themes, is that a post-Christendom Christianity, if it is
to have any positive influence with intelligent and informed people, will require a renewed intellectual appreciation of the Bible
on the part of disciples — one which reveres the Scriptures as
integral to our identity as Christians, but which is equally committed to an unflinching critical appraisal of all its constituent
parts. Biblicism really must be avoided, on the one hand, for
the sake of our credibility before a watchful world, and on the
other, because it ultimately dishonors God and misidentifies the
community of believers.

We need to read the Bible "like any other book," the Victo-
rian Master of Balliol College, Benjamin Jowett, wisely advised,
so that we might rediscover in our own age why it is truly "unlike
any other book." He goes on, in the quotation given above, to
make a comment suitable for serious reflection. The Bible, he
says, when critically interpreted by those who do so carefully and
caringly, not those who merely have a bone to pick with it, "will
be a spirit and not a letter; as it was in the beginning, having an

influence like that of the spoken word, or the book newly found."
So, it isn't a Bible "in the spirit of the Koran" that Christians honestly need, but a Bible that will become for us "a spirit and not
a letter." We will surely need that wise and reasonable spirit in
the post-Christendom age whenever we approach or present to
others our Scriptures.

II.

Before we can speak about that "spirit" of the Bible, though, we
should look more closely at the shape of its "body" — its "table
of contents." Considering the Christian Bible specifically (not
the version of the Hebrew Bible of Judaism), we should be aware
of the fact that neither the Old Testament (whether in its somewhat differing Orthodox, Catholic, or Protestant versions) nor
the New Testament is a slapdash, thrown-together collection of
texts. There is a reason why the shape of each of the canons is as
it is, and why the organization of each mirrors the organization
of the other. In other words, the two canons' tables of contents,
when placed side by side, tell us something important about the
structure of the Christian Bible as a whole. Viewed as a diptych,
the twofold canon suggests an integrated single message to anyone scanning it carefully.

To understand what the Bible is about, then, we have to begin
by asking questions regarding that diptychal canon. *Why these
books, and not others that might have been included? Why do some
of these books seem to contradict, or at least "debate with," other
books in the canon? What is the relationship between the Testaments, and how does the New affect our reading of the Old? Why
are the books ordered as they are, and does the order itself mean
anything?* And so on. The longer we explore the subject, we could

discover, among a great many other things, two aspects in partic-ular that are vital but rarely highlighted in overviews of the Bible:

- first, that the Bible reflects an evolutionary process, and,

- second, that the shape of the canon is directly related to the self-understanding of the community — it is a matter of com-munal identity and continuity.

We will take these one at a time, and then suggest how an un-derstanding of these two aspects of the biblical canon can aid an intelligent and reverent interpretation of it today. This will not be an in-depth study or a historical survey of the development of the canon. In fact, I intend to keep these remarks as uncomplicated and basic as possible. All I wish to do is to present here a few general notes about the character of the canon as Christians in particular have received it. Differences between versions of the canon (between the Hebrew Masoretic text and the Greek Sep-tuagint, for instance, or between the Catholic, Orthodox, Protes-tant, and Ethiopian canons) will be left unaddressed, as will any number of other details about this subject.

THE BIBLE REFLECTS AN EVOLUTIONARY PROCESS

A "flat" reading of the Bible involves, among other things, a fail-ure to see that there is an evolution of thinking about God that takes place within it. The unfolding of biblical revelation is ob-servable in the Old Testament in particular. We should bear in mind that the Old Testament was composed and edited over a period of centuries, roughly spanning a thousand years. (By com-parison, the New Testament was composed over a space of only five decades at most.)

During that long period there was a great development within Judaism, frequently the result of its history and interaction — not often pleasant — with other cultures (particularly Egyptian, Canaanite, Philistine, Babylonian, Assyrian, Persian, Greek, and — beginning in the age of the Maccabees — Roman). Israel's evolving understanding of God can be seen in internal "debates," if you will, between biblical writers. To put it concisely, there is a maturation in the Hebrew Bible's depiction of God — from YHWH being perceived as a tribal deity to his being perceived as a universal one, from God being understood as an anthropomorphic deity (and even a fallible one: he can "repent" of previous decisions he has made — e.g., Gen. 6:6; 1 Sam. 15:11) to being understood as the almighty Lord of heaven and earth, and from "henotheism" ("our" God — supreme and the chief of gods — is nevertheless one god among others) to "monotheism" (there exists only one God, and there are no others).

To illustrate what I'm getting at here, let me bring up a memory from my years in college near Baltimore. There has always been a vigorous "debating" tradition among rabbis, especially over matters of Torah, right up to the present day. I recall watching with interest, during my time at the University of Maryland Baltimore County (UMBC), as Orthodox Jewish students destined for the rabbinate would sometimes gather outside the Political Science Building on warm afternoons and argue among themselves — furiously at times — over this or that detail of Talmudic law. This wasn't quarreling; there was no coming to blows or real anger, no matter how energetic and loud the discussion could become at times. This was just hashing out things in a long-accustomed way. Such heated debate has been a feature of Jewish faith for millennia; and even debating with God is not off-limits in Jewish piety. It's a mark of their living faith, communal identity, and personal engagement.

It shouldn't surprise us, then, that the most sacred of Jewish texts reveals a similar Jewish characteristic. The Bible is a book in which a lot of hashing out takes place over many generations. Again, the Old Testament isn't a flat text. Jews hold the first five books, those "of Moses," to be "the word of God" in a way that the rest of the Old Testament is not. The other canonical writings carry on the word of God, but they don't carry the same weight of authority, nor are they regarded as "the word of God" in the same way that the Pentateuch is. (This, as we shall see, is mirrored in the New Testament with the special reverence accorded the Four Gospels in classical Christianity — which is why, by ages-old custom, one stands at attention when the Gospels are read aloud at the Eucharistic liturgy, a practice not expected in that context for readings from other biblical books.)

Just two examples will make the point. One internal "debate" in the Old Testament involves what I have called elsewhere "conventional piety."[1] Since I've gone into some detail on that issue in my first book, *Knowing Darkness,* I won't belabor the point here. It is enough to say that a hallmark of Old Testament "conventional piety" — what can be seen in, for instance, the book of Proverbs (another classic expression is Psalm 37) — is the idea that God rewards righteous behavior and punishes evildoers during their lives. The problem, of course, is that it is frequently the case that the good suffer and the wicked prosper, and so later generations of Wisdom writers dealt with those obvious facts of life head-on. The authors of Job and Ecclesiastes in particular mimicked texts of conventional piety found in earlier Wisdom writers, only to turn the tables and challenge directly the very grounds of such naïve biblical platitudes. (In Job, the speeches of Job's friends

1. See *Knowing Darkness: On Skepticism, Melancholy, Friendship, and God* (Grand Rapids: Wm. B. Eerdmans, 2009), Chapter Five, "Job and the Problem of Conventional Piety," pp. 73-95.

are full of conventionally pious sentiments, some of them taken almost verbatim from other biblical Wisdom books, only to be countered by Job and even God himself; in Ecclesiastes, to cite but one instance, one might note what I take to be the intended contradiction of 8:12-13 and 8:14.) Obviously, neither of these astringent books repudiated morality, righteousness, or the holiness of God; but they took the argument to a different and more sophisticated level entirely. Overall, we have a debate of existential issues in the Wisdom books of the Old Testament; and the fact that, alongside Psalms and Proverbs, such countervailing and straightforwardly disturbing books as Job and Ecclesiastes also made the final cut should signal us that the canon is not a uniform text with a single, flat moral and theological viewpoint.

Another example of an internal canonical debate in the Old Testament regards the proper attitude the Jewish people should have towards Gentiles — even their most notable enemies. To see this, one can contrast the harsh approach in Ezra 9 and 10 toward those who had married Gentile wives after the Babylonian exile, and Ezra's insistence that the wives be sent packing, with the irenic book of Ruth (a late book in the canon), in which the heroine and great-grandmother of King David is revealed to have been a Moabite woman. Moabites, it should be recalled, were detested Gentiles, even said to be the fruit of the abomination of incest (Gen. 19:30-38).

Or, one might contrast the sheer glee with which the prophet Nahum describes the historical destruction of Assyrian Nineveh in 612 B.C. with the parabolic irony of the book of Jonah toward that same deeply hated Gentile city many years later. There was certainly no love on Nahum's (or most Jews') part for the brutal Assyrians. The latter, after all, had destroyed the Northern Kingdom of Israel with extraordinary savagery in the 720s B.C., and had deported (in a cruel forced march) the survivors.

The book of Jonah, for its part, is one of the latest books of the Hebrew canon, written three hundred years or more after the fall of the Northern Kingdom. It is a parable, a "what if" story. In this case, it asks the question "*What if* the Assyrian Ninevites had repented?" Jonah is a comic work, with the only unpleasant person in the story being the disobedient prophet (a parody of those who, like Ezra many years before, had nothing but disdain for all Gentiles?). All around the prophet Jonah in the story, from the pagans onboard the ship who regretfully cast him into the deep (1:16) to the hateful Ninevites themselves (3:5-10), Gentiles keep turning to God, and God shows them kindness and mercy — much to the chagrin of the petulant and bloodthirsty prophet. Jonah rebukes God angrily, sulking like a spoiled brat, because God proves merciful (4:2-3). This gem of a book ends with a baited hook of a question really intended for the reader. In essence it asks, "Will you be merciful as God is, or will you be a bitter and angry hater like Jonah?" This is not only a question about the character of the audience, but a repudiation of those views about God that would depict him as hating Gentiles or desiring to judge and destroy them. Even the most dreaded Gentiles, like the Assyrians, stand a chance with God.

So, against Ezra, there is Ruth; against Nahum, Jonah. The internal canonical debate, then, hashes out what sort of God it is whom Israel worships, and, along with that great concern, what sort of people should those who worship him be as a consequence.

Turning to Christian readers, logically the Old Testament can only be viewed as a *progressive revelation.* It is progressing toward what the Christian believes to be a fuller revealing of God, his definitive self-disclosure. "Truly, I say to you, many prophets and righteous men longed to see what you see, and did not see it, and to hear what you hear, and did not hear it" (Matt. 13:17).

The statements of Jesus in the Sermon on the Mount, in which he says "You have heard that it was said . . . but I say to you" (Matt. 5:21-22, 27-28, 31-32, 33-34, 38-39, 43-44), should be appreciated by the disciple for the claims of superior revelation that they are. Jesus means that he corrects all previous misconceptions about God's way. He sets himself up as the definitive interpreter of Torah, the one who fulfills ("brings to fullness" or "completes") "the law and the prophets" (Matt. 5:17). Without him, in other words, the Old Testament is inconclusive. He points his followers to the spirit of righteousness, not to the letter of the Law. The Gospel of John, going further along these lines, says of Jesus that he is "the Word of God" who "became flesh," and that he alone "has made [God] known" fully (John 1:1, 14, 18). The word "known" in John 1:18 is actually *exegesato* — "exegeted." This is the same word we use when we speak of interpreting — "reading out of" or "exegeting" — a text, be it a biblical text or any other written source. Like an otherwise indecipherable text, then, God has been *exegeted* — *interpreted* — to us by Jesus, who is the enfleshed "Word," the perfect interpreter and interpretation both.

The Christian, looking back over the Old Testament, views it as a vast landscape of highs and lows. It isn't flat tableland, but a terrain with various features — many that are exquisitely beautiful and some that are frankly unsightly. It is, to use a different analogy, like a family photograph album. If I sit and open up the family photos, I can see myself as an infant. A few pages on, I'm a toddler, then a young boy, then a teenager, and then a young man, and — if I'm old enough — there I am as a man with a family and a career and graying temples. The meaning should be clear. The Old Testament is uneven, and it depicts — like a series of pictures taken over a long stretch of years — a slow progression toward greater maturity and comprehension. When I look at myself in the family album, I can remember my failures as well as my successes as I grew up. At age seven, I understood my parents and teachers according to the age limitations of a seven-year-old, but by age seventeen my understanding had changed considerably — and pictures from those days show it. Again, in maturity, I can see things about my parents I could never have understood as a boy — their lives, their hopes and wishes, their desires for my life. The pictures indicate my maturation over time. The Old Testament gives us pictures, if you will, of the maturation, not of God, but of Israel and its insights about God — the broadening of the communal mind.

The Old Testament depicts an evolution, then. For the Christian, who looks back over the Old Testament from the vantage point of Jesus and his kingdom, the inscrutable God of "Second" Isaiah, say, or the merciful God of the book of Jonah, is a much more evolved understanding of God than are, say, earlier depictions in which he is conceived as ordering his people to kill Canaanites or to stone Sabbath-breakers to death. To put it bluntly, the Christian — enlightened by Christ and the morality of the kingdom — should never accept the violence and bloodshed of the Old Testament as anything but a misconception of God. Early Fathers of the Church, following the model set by Jewish theologians such as the first-century Philo of Alexandria, dealt with this difficulty by choosing to allegorize morally offensive texts. Twice in his *Monastic Rule,* just to pick one from among countless patristic examples, Benedict of Nursia interprets Psalm 137's concluding curse upon the Babylonians — "Happy shall he be who takes your little ones and dashes them against the rock!" (v. 9) — as meaning the dashing of his monks' small, "immature" sins against the rock of Christ. Allegorizing unpleasant passages may have worked well enough in a pre-critical age, but today the same approach can only lead to exegetical complications and absurdities (not that that has discouraged some from trying it). But it is far more sensible in our age simply to admit that such passages illustrate a primitive — and ultimately wrongheaded — portrayal of God, one corrected by later Old Testament writers and, finally, by Jesus. The internal "debate" is better acknowledged than not. There is nothing wrong about recognizing scriptural contradictions when they occur. It's honest; and it's a reminder that these contradictions serve the purposes of developing insight and maturity. When looked at as a debate, the Bible's contradictions should be expected and not problematic. It's only when one regards the Bible as a flat text, and every part equally true, that contradictions seem a threat, and the difficulties for any sane appreciation of the Bible insurmountable.

A Biblicist likely would demur at all this. How can I say such things without demeaning God's book? What gives me the right to claim that the biblical picture of God "evolves"? Isn't the Bible "the word of God"?

Again, emphatically, no; the Bible is not "the word of God" — Jesus definitively is "the Word of God" for the Christian. The Bible is "the word of God" only insofar as it leads toward Jesus, and it is a word that is corrected by the standard of Jesus' own teachings. The Biblicist wants a "monophysite" Bible — a Bible of just "one nature," one that is all divine, with no human element in it. But the Bible is a human product before all else, written by men, edited, arranged, and rearranged, with numerous variants throughout the copies of its texts, and so forth. It is only "divine" in the sense that — so we believe — God breathed enough truth through its authors that it has a living effect on us. Our faith is in the God who infinitely transcends the texts, not in the particular, fragile words of those texts themselves.

There are passages in the New Testament that lead us to understand that Christians in the early years of the faith looked upon the Old Testament revelation in such a way. Paul provides the most obvious, and most extreme, example of this. In 2 Corinthians 3, for instance, he compares the two testaments in stark contrast, his most telling statement in the passage perhaps being this one: We apostles are, he says, "ministers of a new covenant, not in a written code [literally, "word"] but in the Spirit; for the written code ["word"] kills, but the Spirit gives life" (v. 6). The Old Testament, he says, is written "with ink" and "on tablets of stone" (v. 3); it is a "dispensation of death" (v. 7) and a "dispensation of condemnation" (v.9), and it will "fade away" (v. 11). These are very tough words indeed. And, in contrast, the gospel of Christ is written "with the Spirit of the living God" and "on tablets of human [literally "fleshly"] hearts" (v. 3); it is "a dispensation of the Spirit . . . with greater splendor" (v. 8), and it is "permanent" (v. 11). What's more, the Old Covenant cannot be unveiled and properly understood without recourse to the New Covenant in Christ (vv. 12-18). In Galatians, we find Paul once again making a sustained argument in chapters 3 and 4 along similar lines. The Law of Moses, he says straightforwardly, is inferior to the gospel. Paul allows that the Law is that which leads to Christ (3:24), but then it retreats before Christ's higher teaching. Paul makes the same point in Romans 10:4, where he writes, "For Christ is the end ["goal"] of the law." When he writes in Galatians 3:19 that the Law "was ordained by angels through an intermediary [i.e., Moses]," he is saying that the transmission of it had not come directly from God, but indirectly — passed through intermediate hands (angelic and human agency) before being received by Israel. The implication is that, though good, the Law isn't utterly reliable. Nor is it Paul alone who makes such comparisons of Old and New. Similar assessments of earlier scriptural revelation can be found throughout the New Testament.

The point here, however, is not that we should read Paul or the New Testament any less critically than we do the Old Testament.

It is only to note that Paul's perspective regarding the biblical Torah, though it is the most radical in the New Testament, illustrates most strikingly for us the problem of reading the Bible as a flat text. Paul himself didn't read it that way. He was not a fundamentalist, not a Biblicist. Paul reads the Old Testament with the critical mind of a first-century rabbi, like his contemporary Philo. He frequently prefers a "spiritual" (allegorical) reading to a strictly literal reading of a given text, thus avoiding the difficulties that a literalistic reading would present. All the New Testament writers, it can be said, assume that there was an evolution in the biblical revelation, culminating in Christ. None of them are fundamentalists or Biblicists in the modern sense.

This brings us to the second aspect of the canon that I wish to highlight here, and to the New Testament in particular.

THE SHAPE OF THE CANON IS DIRECTLY RELATED TO THE SELF-UNDERSTANDING OF THE COMMUNITY

Like the Old Testament, the New Testament reflects the community that gave it its shape. Unlike the Old Testament, however, it is made up of texts written over a period of just fifty years, the earliest dating to A.D. 52, and the latest probably to the decade before 100. However, although it is comprised of first-century books, in its developed form it reveals the identity of a fourth-century church. More specifically still, what we have inherited is a "Roman" canon, a "Petrine" and "Pauline" canon, and its twenty-seven books are arranged accordingly.

The writings in the New Testament include occasional letters (those by, and those attributed to, Paul, James, Peter, John, and Jude), what appear to be written general exhortations or sermons to churches (Hebrews and 1 John; but possibly also James and 1 Peter), four gospels, a "novelistic" book of history (Acts) — written, it seems, because the last of the first generation were passing away — and a single, concluding apocalypse. Apart from these texts, we have no other Christian writings that can be dated with confidence to the first century.[2] That the New Testament texts were collected and preserved from a very early date seems obvious, showing that they were accounted precious. Already in the first century Paul's letters were being read in some churches as scripture. The Second Letter of Peter, possibly the latest of our New Testament books, says so explicitly: "So also our beloved brother Paul wrote to you according to the wisdom given him, speaking of this as he does in all his letters. There are some things hard in them to understand, which the ignorant and unstable twist to their own destruction, *as they do the other scriptures*" (3:15-16; emphasis mine). From the beginning, then, the canon was forming. And also from the beginning, as this snippet from 2 Peter reveals, there were evidently "right" and "wrong" ways to read the same texts.

In addition to "ignorant and unstable twisting" of presumably genuine apostolic writings (although 2 Peter itself was certainly not a genuine work of that apostle — pseudonymous authorship not necessarily being frowned upon in the ancient world), there were, during the second and third centuries, numerous other writings being produced, many of them bearing names of first-century apostles. Some of these later works would be deemed orthodox and even canonical in various churches, some would be read devotionally but never treated seriously as canon, and still others would represent alternative canons in what would be later viewed as heterodox churches.

2. Still, it is possible that, among the writings of the Apostolic Fathers, the *Didache* might be dated that early; and, while the *Gospel of Thomas* in the Coptic version found at Nag Hammadi is a much later text, the older Greek version, of which only late-third-century fragments exist, might be of first-century provenance.

One of the chief purposes of having an "orthodox" canon of writings, it should be recalled, was precisely to distinguish between orthodoxy and heterodoxy, truth and falsehood, and authenticity and non-authenticity. The content of the New Testament, as it took shape, was based on whether or not the texts in question came from Christian *antiquity* (i.e., datable to the first century), and thus were considered to be *apostolic* in origin, or at least written by someone close to an apostle (thus, for instance, Mark on behalf of Peter, Luke on behalf of Paul); whether or not the texts were *read widely* as scripture throughout all the churches; and whether or not the texts adhered closely to the universally accepted orthodox *regula fidei*. Antiquity, apostolicity, catholicity, and orthodoxy were thus the four marks of those texts considered worthy of inclusion into the church's canon.

The period from 140 to 200 was decisive for the canon as we now have it, as early Christian writers such as Justin Martyr, Irenaeus of Lyons, Clement of Alexandria, Tertullian, and others make clear. To counter the heresies of the period (Marcion's anti-Jewish one, in particular, which presented what was the first canonical list of first-century apostolic writings), churches in the Roman world felt compelled to draw up lists of approved books for use in their worship. These lists overlapped for the most part, some canons having more books in them and some having less, some including books that our familiar New Testament does not include, and some excluding books that ours contains. Canons could vary from locale to locale, a fact which suggests a more flexible attitude in these centuries toward biblical inspiration than would be the case in the century following. As long as the other guiding norms of the *regula fidei* and apostolically ordained oversight were in place, it seems a more open-ended outlook was possible between regional churches.

The fourth century, of course, altered things in a way that continues to the present day. With Constantine and his heirs had come a typically orderly Roman expectation that there must be one church, a uniform creedal orthodoxy, a unified episcopate, and one Bible used throughout the empire. (That was their wish, at any rate, even though the reality was never quite so tidy as all that.)

It was during the latter half of this momentous age that the canon of the New Testament as we have it today became fixed, in effect "closed." No council of the church decided this officially at the time. That was to occur for the first time at the Council of Trent of the Roman Catholic Church in the sixteenth century (!). The first list we have that contains the twenty-seven books of our New Testament comes from Athanasius, Patriarch of Alexandria. It was the custom for that patriarch to write an encyclical to the churches under his oversight each year in preparation for the Easter celebration. In his thirty-ninth such letter, that of 367, he lists the canonical books of both testaments, though the New Testament books are (significantly) not given in the same order as we have them. The letters of James, Peter, John, and Jude immediately follow Acts, for example, and then come the Pauline epistles. These books only, he writes, "are the fountains of salvation," and no one is "to add to these, [or] . . . take aught from these." He lists, as well, other writings that the Fathers recommend as useful and instructive; but he sternly warns against heretical writings that "beguile" and "lead astray." In short, this list is poised to stand against heretical writings on the one hand, and to be a reliable standard by which to measure the worth of other orthodox writings on the other.[3]

When Athanasius composed this letter, his "see" (or "seat"

3. Philip Schaff, D.D., LL.D., and Henry Wace, D.D., *A Select Library of the Christian Church: Nicene and Post-Nicene Fathers (Second Series), Volume 4: Athanasius: Select Works and Letters* (Peabody, Mass.: Hendrickson Publishers, 1999), pp. 551-52.

— a term indicating a bishop's throne, and thus his authority) in Alexandria was one of the three great "Petrine" sees of the empire. The other two were Rome and Antioch in Syria, with Rome taking the primacy among them. These three sees claimed, one way or another, a vital association with the apostle Peter, upon whose person and extraordinary conviction, it was believed, the church had been built (Matt. 16:17-19). To these three apostolic sees were later added in importance that of Constantinople, and finally that of Jerusalem.

For the early church, Peter was a sure sign and touchstone of apostolic tradition. It was around the central figure of Peter that other apostolic figures (Paul and John, for example) and their writings were gathered and, in a sense, found their legitimacy. This was a development in the church's understanding of itself and what constituted its authentic doctrine. Let me be clear at this point: I am not referring to the papacy. There was no "papacy" as it exists today during the early centuries of the church. There was a primacy accorded to the church in Rome, not simply because Rome was the imperial seat (although, of course, that was hardly a negligible factor), but because it was there that the most important apostles, Peter and Paul, had met their deaths. The Roman church was multifaceted in the first century, under numerous "overseers" and "elders" ("bishops" and/or "priests"), and made up of various congregations throughout the city. The foundation of genuineness and the source for unity between them, it would seem, was the shared heritage of Peter and Paul, with Peter's status being the more significant due to his personal friendship with Jesus. This would, in time, be applied to the development of the Roman see, and — with the loss of the other great Petrine sees to Islam, and with the schism between Rome and Constantinople in 1066 — Rome would emerge as the sole Petrine see in the West, and the papacy would come into its own.

It is the threefold fourth-century emphasis on Peter, Paul, and Rome that concerns us here, because it concerns the shape the New Testament canon would take finally and permanently for all Christians.

It was the Latin Vulgate that settled the ordering of the New Testament's table of contents for all Bibles ever since. Commissioned by Pope Damasus I in 382, and largely the work of the brilliant, and notoriously irascible and mercurial, Jerome, it became the standard Latin translation of the Bible. The New Testament books were the same as those listed in Athanasius's Festal Letter of 367, reflecting the same agreed-upon canon of imperial Christendom. But the Vulgate reordered the books so that, for instance, the letters of Paul preceded the "Catholic" epistles, instead of the other way around, with the Letter to the Romans conspicuously heading the list of collected apostolic letters. The Vulgate's table of contents, it might therefore be noticed, not only reflected "Rome" in the broad sense of the whole empire, east and west; it also reflected more narrowly the Eternal City herself, in addition to the legacy of Peter and Paul.

In the Christian Bible as well, the Old Testament's order of books had developed along different lines than those of the Hebrew. Instead of the latter's tripartite division (the five books of Moses, the prophets, and the "writings"), the Christian Old Testament was divided into four sections: the five books of Moses, the historical books, the books of poetry and wisdom, and the prophets. The New Testament canon corresponds to this, with its similar fourfold division into four gospels (= five books of Moses), one historical book (Acts), the "wisdom" of the apostles' epistles, and one book of prophecy (Revelation). The identification, then, of the New Testament's scriptures as both continuation and supersession of the Old Testament's is indicated by the "mirroring" canonical shapes of their contents, the diptychal canon I referred to above. The first thing to note, then, is that the Christian Bible fully acknowledges Christianity's Jewish origins, including the sacred books of its mother faith.

To go a step further in our endeavor to understand the New Testament canon in its final, fourth century, Roman shape, we can tick off the following points: First, it establishes legitimate, original doctrinal boundaries. Second, it identifies the community and its heritage as the church that Christ himself began. Third, it traces the church as its center shifted geographically and influentially from Jerusalem to the imperial capital, Rome, from whence it continued to spread to the end of the earth (cf. Acts 1:8). Fourth, it stresses the roles in that movement played by Rome's two pre-eminent apostles, Peter and Paul. We will take these one at a time.

First, it establishes legitimate, original doctrinal boundaries. The New Testament groups together a generously wide range of first-century texts. We have become so accustomed to having them side by side that we sometimes fail to notice how very different these texts are in relation to each other in numerous ways. The Christology of Mark is not that of John's Gospel, for instance, and neither is it that of Hebrews. This is not to say, obviously, that they are in conflict, but that they are in creative tension; and only a liberal inclusiveness would have deemed it appropriate to put such distinct perspectives into a single canon.[4] The boundaries of orthodoxy, then, were not narrow, but wide enough to embrace Mark and John, Luke and Revelation, Paul and James. All these, in their various ways, gave meat and vitality to the bare bones of the Creed.

4. A fine introduction to the variety of Christologies to be found in the New Testament is Raymond E. Brown's book, *An Introduction to New Testament Christology* (Mahwah, N.J.: Paulist Press, 1994).

Second, it identifies the community and its heritage as the church that Christ himself began. This is established in the very first Gospel in the canon, and it is the reason why Matthew was recognized from the very beginning as "the ecclesiastical Gospel" and also why — as the canon developed under the auspices of the "Petrine" sees — it was placed prominently at the head of the canon. What is the church? Who are these people who proclaim that Jesus is Lord and Christ? The answer to these questions about the Christian community's identity begins to take shape in the very first text in the canon to use the word "church": "And I tell you, you are Peter, and on this rock I will build my church . . ." (Matt. 16:18). The church, then, is that community which Jesus established with Peter. And Peter's churches were first among the churches, just as Peter himself had stood as the "first" *(protos)* among the Twelve to whom Jesus had given apostolic authority (Matt. 10:1-4). Peter's primacy is a given in Matthew, and the church's identity as the original church, built by Christ, cannot be dissociated from him as its foundation.

And this brings us to the third and fourth points concerning the canon that I wish to mention, which we must take together. So —

Third, it traces the church as its center shifted geographically and influentially from Jerusalem to the imperial capital, Rome, from whence it continued to spread to the end of the earth (cf. Acts 1:8). And, *fourth, it stresses the roles in that movement played by Rome's two pre-eminent apostles, Peter and Paul.* With these two statements in mind, then, here is a quick overview of the shape of the New Testament as it comes to us filtered through the Petrine sees of Rome, Antioch, and Alexandria, and, finally, through the Latin Roman see and its authoritative Vulgate version.

THE SHAPE OF THE NEW TESTAMENT

The Four Gospels: Matthew, Mark, Luke, and John

As we noted above, Matthew takes the lead. Composed, it seems most likely, in Antioch, it is the Gospel most concerned to clarify the church's identity, with Peter as the rallying point and foundation stone, his apostolic status being that of the "first" among equals. This would have legitimated, in the minds of early Christians, the roles of the sees of Antioch, Rome, and Alexandria, who derived their authority from Peter, either directly or (as in the case of Alexandria) through one of his closest disciples (in Alexandria's case, the evangelist John Mark).

Matthew, then, having based the church's identity on the person and message of Peter, is followed by the Gospel of Peter himself — because, as the earliest Fathers (Irenaeus, for example) tell us, Mark merely put down in writing what Peter had proclaimed.

Alongside Peter stands Paul in the early Roman Christian and canonical mind, the other apostle who was martyred in the Eternal City; and so Luke, the Third Gospel, is the Gospel of Paul, for Luke was that apostle's great companion. The Gospel of Luke is only one half of a two-part work, with the book of Acts being the second half (together, Luke–Acts is the *Iliad* and the *Odyssey* of the New Testament, if you will); but the canon divides these two halves and inserts between them the Fourth Gospel, that attributed to John.

This very different Gospel, having the highest Christology of all in the New Testament and considered "the spiritual Gospel" by the early church, crowns the other three. But it concludes — as Matthew's began, so to speak — with the re-establishing of Peter and his authority, along with a prophecy concerning his death (which every reader knew had occurred, by crucifixion, in Rome):

Feed my sheep [i.e., be the Shepherd of my people]. Truly, truly, I say
to you, when you were young, you girded yourself and walked where
you would; but when you are old, you will stretch out your hands, and
another will gird you and carry you where you do not wish to go. . . .
Follow me. (John 21:17-19)

So, the Four Gospels, in addition to recording the acts and
words of Jesus, also identify the church as that founded upon
Peter, whose gospel — along with that of Paul, his spiritual if not
his actual companion in ministry — is the true, apostolic one,
and whose words continue to feed the sheep as sustenance from
a good shepherd of Christ's flock.

The Book of the Acts of the Apostles

Acts continues, as said above, the Gospel of Luke. Although it
tells of the Twelve, including the replacement of Judas the traitor
with Matthias, and the leadership of James, the Lord's brother, as
well as others (Stephen, Philip, Barnabas, Mark, Silas, and Timothy), its two great heroes are Peter and Paul. Peter's story is told
through chapter twelve, and he reappears at the council in Jerusalem in chapter fifteen. Paul's story begins near the end of chapter
seven, at the stoning of Stephen, and ends with him in Rome, proclaiming the kingdom of God. And there it concludes. Although
Acts was written after the martyrdoms of both Peter and Paul, it
ends on a note of triumph and doesn't speak of their deaths.

Note, then, not only the biographical aspect of Acts, but also
the geographical aspect (and keep it in mind when we come to
the book of Revelation). Acts 1:8 had set the trajectory: "You shall
be my witnesses in Jerusalem and in all Judea and Samaria and
to the end of the earth." Rome, where the book concludes (after
recounting the apostles' work in Jerusalem, Judea, and Samaria),
is in fact the jumping-off point for "the end of the earth." What

Acts recounts is how the center of the church's gravity shifted from Jerusalem to Rome. The author, who wrote about a decade or so after the fact, knew well that Jerusalem's church had disappeared from that city during the Roman conquest in 71.

Acts, then, is about Peter, Paul, and Rome, about the triumphant proclamation of the kingdom of God (Acts 28:31 — the book's concluding verse!) in Rome, through Paul's teaching, which — in essence — is the teaching of Jesus, and of Peter as well.

The Epistles of Paul: Romans, 1 and 2 Corinthians, Galatians, Ephesians, Philippians, Colossians, 1 and 2 Thessalonians, 1 and 2 Timothy, Titus, Philemon, and Hebrews

Before proceeding further, it's necessary to say beforehand that the "Pauline corpus" is made up of books that are genuinely by Paul, some that are disputed, and some that clearly are not by the historical Paul. Romans, the two letters to the Corinthians, Galatians, Philippians, 1 Thessalonians, and Philemon are indisputably by Paul. Ephesians, Colossians, and 2 Thessalonians are disputed. (I tend to think that the last is genuine, and the other two are not.) The Pastoral Epistles (the two to Timothy and Titus) are almost certainly not, and Hebrews was only accorded Pauline authorship with ambivalence at most from the earliest period (the mention of Paul's companion, Timothy, in 13:23 certainly encouraged the notion of Pauline authorship).[5]

---

5. Many books of worth come to mind for an introductory study of Paul. Here I will mention only three. For a collection of translated primary texts and valuable essays, it is hard to top *The Writings of St. Paul: A Norton Critical Edition* (Second Edition), edited by Wayne A. Meeks and John T. Fitzgerald (New York: W. W. Norton, 2007). For a fine exploration of the Pauline texts' meaning, their historical background, and supporting archaeological evidence, I recommend *In Search of Paul: How Jesus' Apostle Opposed Rome's Empire with God's Kingdom,* by John Dominic Crossan and Jonathan L. Reed

This isn't the place to discuss the common ancient practice of pseudonymous authorship, except to note that it was not viewed as inappropriate or immoral, and it certainly wasn't intended to fool anybody. It carried on the tradition, it was believed, of the one under whose name such a text was written, sometimes for polemical reasons (as, for example, in the Pastoral Epistles, which appear to oppose an exaggerated asceticism espoused in some Pauline churches with a much more conservative version of Pauline Christianity). It was a practice that, in some aspects, resembles the later papal custom of issuing encyclicals under the name, and with the authority, of Peter (the "Apostolic See"). But we are only concerned here with the Pauline corpus as a constituent part of the canon.

In this light, we notice that — unlike other arrangements of the New Testament canon — the Vulgate puts Romans at the head, right after Acts. By putting the texts in this order, we find Acts concluding with Paul preaching the gospel in Rome, and then we move directly to the epistle in which he fleshes out that gospel to the church in that very city (and even defines the kingdom of God, mentioned in Acts 28:31, with Romans 14:17).

In geographical terms, the Pauline corpus moves from Rome and the West eastward, retracing Paul's journeys through Greece and Asia Minor, and concluding on the outskirts, if you will, of Jerusalem with the Letter (or perhaps it might better be called the Homily) to the Hebrews. In this way, we can note that the center of authoritative gravity has shifted to Rome from Jerusalem ("Those who come from Italy send you greetings"; Heb. 13:24).

Hebrews ends on a rather poignant note, with the exhortation

(New York: HarperOne, 2005). Another useful little book is *Paul: A Very Short Introduction,* by E. P. Sanders (New York: Oxford University Press, 2001).

to "remember your leaders, those who spoke to you the word of God; consider the outcome of their life, and imitate their faith" (13:7). Hebrews 13:9 ("it is well that the heart be strengthened by grace, not by foods, which have not benefited their adherents" — referring to matters of "foods" in Jewish law) even echoes faintly Paul's words in Romans 14:17 ("For the kingdom of God is not meat and drink" — again, referring to Jewish regulations concerning food), thus bringing such tense early Jewish Christian concerns full circle. It goes on to call Hebrew Christians to leave behind the synagogues that have repudiated them: "We have an altar from which those who serve the tent have no right to eat. . . . Therefore let us go forth to him outside the camp, and bear the abuse he endured" (13:10-13).

The "Catholic" Epistles:
James, 1 and 2 Peter, 1, 2, and 3 John, and Jude

In his letter to the Galatians, Paul speaks (in not the most flattering terms, admittedly, though certainly not in any directly derogatory way) of the "pillars" of the church in Jerusalem, whom he lists in this order: "James and Cephas [i.e., "Peter"] and John" (2:9). It is therefore no coincidence that, after Hebrews (and almost picking up where Hebrews left off in its opening address "to the twelve tribes in the Dispersion"), we have the Letter of James, followed by the letters of Peter and John — in that order. And then, almost coming as an afterthought and continuing themes also found in 2 Peter, we have the Letter of Jude, "servant of Jesus Christ and brother of James" (1:1). Jude is placed here, an addendum to the three "pillars" in Jerusalem, because he is the brother of James and thus an extension of his authority, although he is not one of the "pillars" whom Paul lists.

With the Catholic epistles, we have in a sense moved backward, both geographically and chronologically (but canonically, not historically, since these letters are among the latest biblical books to be written), from Rome to Jerusalem the mother church, with its venerable apostolic "pillars," each of whom had known Jesus personally. As already noted, Paul's authority and his "scriptures" are guaranteed by no one less than "Peter" himself (2 Pet. 3:15-16).

The Book of Revelation

The New Testament concludes with a single work of prophecy. Even though scholars make distinctions between "apocalyptic literature" and "prophetic literature," neither Jews nor Christians distinguished between these related, overlapping genres. Just as the Old Testament in the Christian Bible has the prophets positioned as the last section of the canon, so the New Testament has its book of the Revelation ("Apocalypse") to John. One among many early Christian and Jewish apocalypses, the canonical worthiness of Revelation was long disputed. Athanasius seems to have been the one who decided finally in its favor, including it in his canonical list in 367. The reason for its inclusion, after Constantine's (and Julian the Apostate's) reign, may have been largely because it was understood to be partially fulfilled by the imperial embrace of Christianity: "The kingdom of the world has become the kingdom of our Lord and of his Christ, and he shall reign for ever and ever" (11:15).

Revelation may be viewed as taking the New Testament trajectory to its ultimate destination. If Acts took the church from Jerusalem to Rome (and "to the end of the earth"), Revelation takes it from Rome to the New Jerusalem.

So, with Revelation, the fourth-century canon not only looks back at the church's past, but also (as it understands it in light of the "Constantinian Privilege") looks at its present, and finally toward its future.

III.

"When interpreted like any other book, by the same rules of ev-idence and the same canons of criticism, the Bible will still re-main unlike any other book," wrote Benjamin Jowett. Doubtless, he was right about that. It certainly cannot reasonably be read, as Dean Inge put it, "in the spirit of the Koran"; and yet Biblicists read it in a way very close to that. Increasingly, that approach can be seen to be untenable and misleading. One of the greatest barriers to Christian faith today, at least among those for whom reason and spiritual integrity, not to say depth, are imperative, is the incredible idea of an "inerrant" or "infallible" Bible, if by these terms we mean a book that is completely factual and fault-less in every detail, including its "science" and historiography. As indicated above, when held up to the standard of the teachings of Jesus, it is not even beyond criticism in many of its primitive and disturbing representations of God. We may say, reasonably enough, that the Bible "infallibly" (i.e., "unfailingly") leads us, as an evolving revelation, to the person of Jesus, and to God. But if we stop here or there along its Old Testament trajectory, we may find it fallible at many particular points, though its advance is still infallibly pointing ahead to a decisive endpoint. Only the movement itself of the trajectory of biblical revelation is un-failing, since it reaches the goal, which is the Word made flesh. Christians stop with Jesus; there alone is the goal and their place to settle. It is precisely there that the course of biblical revelation hits its destined target. There we see the truly infallible aspect of the Bible.

Like dogma, as we discussed it in Chapter Two, the Bible is a signpost — a monumental and vital one — indicating an ex-perience of God that is ours to explore. It is not a flat text or a divine Word in some "Koranic" sense. It is a body of literature, a collection and a library, carefully composed, selected, edited, and arranged by responsible men down long ages, and it requires an equally careful handling and discernment.

So, with the evolution and shape of the Christian canon in mind, as we have briefly described it above, we see that this "book" is something more than a book. Again, in Jowett's words, we have the beginnings of "a picture which is restored after many ages to its original state." That "original state" is nothing less than the *humanity* of it. The Bible is profoundly *human* in its development, its communal origins, and its humbleness of expression. Its evident imperfections should endear it to us more than any theory of its possessing a sort of megalithic divine flawlessness. And, unless we think that there is anything in this estimation of it that is unworthy, it should also be remembered by believers that humans are made "in the image and likeness of God."

Again, Jowett says that, understood correctly, the Bible shall become for us "a spirit and not a letter." This, we might say, is the divine aspect at work. For believers, the revelation is indeed a revelation, an unveiling — not an unveiling of God so much as an unveiling of our minds to God (cf. 1 Cor. 13:8-13; 2 Cor. 3:15-18). These texts become God-spirated "words" that bring to us the Word made flesh — God present within the frailty of the human condition and communicating himself to us in a way that our minds can grasp. That is the essence of our faith — that God exists, and that he has shown himself in Christ, who has taught us the way of life, and rescued us from sin and death. There is the perfection we seek — God, not the Bible. But we thank God for the Bible.

Richard Slotkin has explained "myth" well, saying that for it to be viable it must depend "upon the applicability of its particular terms and metaphors to the peculiar conditions of history and environment that dominate the life of a particular people."[6] By "myth" he doesn't mean that which isn't true, but the "terms and metaphors" that shape our communal perspective of the world, our selves, and the place in the world that we must occupy meaningfully. In other words, myth shapes community and tells us our communal identity. As we have seen, this is what the Christian canon does for the community of Christ's disciples.

But, as we have also seen, its final form is a fourth-century one as well as a first-century one. So it is that, as Christendom gives way to an ever more thoroughly secular order in the West, we retain the Bible that found its definitive shape in the century that gave us Christendom. The two are closely associated, as we have seen. For some, that might appear to present a difficulty. If the Bible is so closely associated with Christendom, how do we dissociate it in our minds from the Christendom that is disappearing? However, I don't believe that this need be seen as a difficulty at all. Christendom only put the final stamp on a process that had been going on for two hundred years before its inception, and the stamp that it put on it was a matter more of canonical ordering than of content. Accordingly, I wish to make the following points.

First, the result of the Christian development of the canon during the second and third centuries, with its rigorously applied criteria of antiquity, apostolicity, catholicity, and orthodoxy, is that our New Testament contains the oldest body of Christian literature in existence, carefully and reverently treasured. That fact alone should cause us to be grateful to those who preserved it, edited it, and copied it down the ages, before and after the advent of Christendom in the fourth century. The church of Christendom gave it its final canonical shape, and we have seen how

6. Richard Slotkin, *Regeneration through Violence: The Mythology of the American Frontier, 1600-1860* (New York: Harper Perennial, 1973), p. 14.

the ordering of the canon reflects that; but the contents of that canon reflect the first century and the beginnings of our faith, and that is the more vital aspect. Christendom is fading, but the Bible remains. In it we find our identity as Christians. We have the "terms and metaphors" of our faith, both in the Old Testament as unfolding revelation, and in the New Testament as apostolic testimony. In these we believe we hear God, breathe in his Spirit, and come near him.

But, *second*, this in no way means that we should read the Bible uncritically. As we have seen above, the Bible is a deeply human book, reflecting its times and people, sometimes reaching heights of insight, and sometimes hitting the depths. We must, as Jowett cautioned, read it like any other book; and that implies reading it as the product of fallible persons.

Once again, our standard is Jesus Christ and his kingdom, not a book. If the book says that God ordered the wiping out of the peoples of Canaan, or delights in the death of our enemies or his, or commands that adulterers are to be stoned to death, we must reply that the Word incarnate has corrected that poor image of God for us through his acts and deeds: God does not will that any should perish, he teaches us to love our enemies, he forgives those taken in the worst of sins, and so on. The Bible is not the last word — Jesus is. And his word trumps even the words we find elsewhere in the Scriptures.

Put starkly — indeed, in almost childish terms — the truth is this: If Moses teaches one thing — say, the punishment of stoning for those who have sinned in specific ways — and Jesus teaches something else quite at odds with Moses, either by his words or by his deeds, we go with Jesus and not Moses. Moses is wrong, and Jesus has corrected him. Once more, the Old Testament is a progressive revelation; we must read it not on its own terms, but on Christ's ("For Christ is the end of the law"; Rom.

10:4). Or, as the Letter to the Hebrews puts it, comparing the Old Testament saints to those who have heard and follow Christ: "God had foreseen something better for us, that apart from us they should not be made perfect [or "brought to fullness" or "to completion"]" (Heb. 11:40).

Nor are we uncritical of the New Testament. As a canon, we recognize, the testament has definite implications owing to its fourth-century Vulgate shape. As individual books, we discover, these twenty-seven invaluable texts contain varied messages, even at times not easily reconciled to one another: they recount the same episodes in Christ's life in different ways; there are differing Christologies; sometimes the apostle Paul (for example) can denounce his rivals unmercifully and in very unloving terms; some of the New Testament books are pseudonymous; some depart from the example of Jesus and the authentic writings of Paul in their treatment of women; the book of Revelation is angry, and — spiritually wounded by the persecutions of Christians in Rome — its author depicts a bloodthirsty warrior Jesus, out for vengeance and power, who does not resemble the tough but gentle Christ of the Gospels . . . and the list could go on. The New Testament requires a critical eye no less than the Old Testament.

So, *third* and finally, all this should dissuade post-Christendom Christians from carrying on the inadequate and erroneous biblicism that still characterizes far too many versions of Christianity today. It is simply untenable and intellectually void. It dishonors the very meaning and value of the Bible itself, and misrepresents it, treating it as a strictly divine book. Its humanity is thereby lost and forgotten, and with it any real affinity with the flesh-and-blood and frequently failing human beings we all are. Biblicism turns the Bible into an answer-book and an inerrant paper pope; and it blinds us to reading it as the companionable collection of documents it is, through the humbleness of which God draws us (with a kind of baby talk, as Calvin said) to the Christ we wish to know. Nearly all the writers and heroes of the Bible are flawed persons — as the Bible itself makes abundantly clear, and at times is at pains to highlight. We do ourselves false if we do not read this great collection with its warts and all, recognizing its brilliance and also its foibles, being shocked by its protagonists, being scandalized by some of their misconceptions of God, and realizing, as it so clearly shows us, how thinking about God can and does mature over time. Just like us, the Bible moves from childishness to greater maturity, from misconceptions to contemplative realizations of divinity. And then we come to Jesus, and the scales fall from our eyes, and the veil is removed from our minds, and we put away childish things. One of the most childish things that should be abandoned is biblicism, mainly because the world is a serious place and it warrants serious engagement by the disciples of Jesus.

What we should wish for, over against a secularism that is increasingly grim and warlike and ugly, are communities of disciples whose sole standard is Jesus Christ. Biblicism, too, can look grim and warlike and ugly; and therefore it offers the world no solution or respite. A religion of harsh moralism, which speaks of God as violent and angry, which is double-mindedly divided between a god of war and punishment and the God of peace and forgiveness — in other words, a flat biblicism — is inherently defective. It is incoherent and unconvincing. Christ offers us love, peace, and the beauty of living in the light of God's grace and mercy. He is the light for those searching, the one who guides us through the wasteland to the city set on a hill.

When we read the Bible in Christ-centered community, we do so intelligently, with understanding and carefulness, and fully aware that perfection lies solely in God — toward whom our Bible directs us along its extended arc. And then, as Jowett said so well, the Bible's "beauty will be freshly seen, as of a picture which is restored after many ages to its original state; it will create a new interest and make for itself a new kind of authority by the life which is in it. It will be a spirit and not a letter; as it was in the beginning, having an influence like that of the spoken word, or the book newly found."

FOUR

SAYING YES TO SACRAMENTAL UNITY, AND NO TO SACRAMENTAL DISUNITY

Love bade me welcome, yet my soul drew back,
Guilty of dust and sin.
But quick-ey'd Love, observing me grow slack
From my first entrance in,
Drew nearer to me, sweetly questioning
If I lack'd any thing.
"A guest," I answer'd, "worthy to be here";
Love said, "You shall be he."
"I, the unkind, ungrateful? Ah, my dear,
I cannot look on thee."
Love took my hand, and smiling did reply,
"Who made the eyes but I?"
"Truth, Lord, but I have marr'd them; let my shame
Go where it doth deserve."
"And know you not," says Love, "who bore the blame?"
"My dear, then I will serve."
"You must sit down," says Love, "and taste my meat."
So I did sit and eat.

George Herbert, *Love (III)*, 1633

I.

Christian belief and practice can be comprehended under the complementary terms *incarnation* and *incorporation*. The communal expressions of these central Christian concepts are the sacraments of baptism and the Eucharist. Christendom as such may disappear, but at the heart of Christian faith and life will remain the creedal dogmas, the Bible, and the two sacraments that reveal and re-enact the essential covenantal relationship between Christ and his disciples, and between the disciples themselves. And incarnation and incorporation are at the very heart of baptism and communion.

By the *Incarnation,* Christians mean that the divine Word assumed full human nature. Though uncreated in his divine nature and encompassing all things, he became part of his material creation, joining himself completely and indivisibly to it. As man he was present *within the creation;* as God, creation was simultaneously *within him,* and it remains now united to his divine life in an inseparable bond of union forever.

The complement to the theme of the Incarnation is that of the *incorporation* of ourselves "into Christ." The word "incorporation" literally means "to be formed into" or "included within" a "body." In the sacrament of baptism, all Christians are identified with, and included in, "the body of Christ." The apostle Paul took this idea quite literally. It is what he meant by his oft-repeated phrase "in Christ." For him it was not a metaphor, but living reality. "Do you not know," he wrote to the Roman Christians, "that all of us who have been baptized into Christ Jesus were baptized into his death? We were buried therefore with him by baptism into death, so that as Christ was raised from the dead by the glory of the Father, we too might walk in newness of life" (Rom. 6:3-4). The mystery of incorporation begins with the sacrament of baptism, as Paul says, and, as he also affirms, it is sustained and realized in the sacrament of the Eucharist: "Because there is one bread, we who are many are one body, for we all partake of the one bread" (1 Cor. 10:17). He further expounds this through his teaching on the church as Christ's body in 1 Corinthians 12 (cf. Rom. 12:4-5; also Eph. 4:14-16; Col. 1:18).

Our incorporation into Christ's body is so real and certain a thing that Colossians asserts that Christians are already, in a sense, living with the ascended Lord in heaven, and possess here and now his resurrected life: "You have died, and your life is hid with Christ in God. When Christ who is our life appears, then you also will appear with him in glory" (Col. 3:3-4; cf. also John 5:24). We are, in fact, so thoroughly and *physically* identified with the person and body of Jesus that Paul can — rather shockingly — warn against sexual immorality by saying that such behavior on our part involves not only *our* bodies, but *Christ's* as well: "Do you not know that your bodies are members of Christ? Shall I therefore take the members of Christ and make them members of a prostitute? Never!" (1 Cor. 6:15). And Paul concludes his argument with the admonition: "So glorify God in your body" (1 Cor. 6:20).

For Paul and his hearers, incorporation meant that Christ assumed not only our "nature" (an abstract category), but, in point of fact, each and every bit of our individual persons. On the cross, Paul and the other New Testament writers agree, Christ even took upon himself our personal sins, which he crucified in his own flesh, annihilating them forever: "Christ redeemed us from the curse of the law, having become a curse for us" (Gal. 3:13). Or, again, Paul writes, bluntly and surprisingly, "For our sake [God] made him to be sin who knew no sin, so that in him we might become the righteousness of God" (2 Cor. 5:21). Theologically, this is the language of both incarnation and incorporation.

All this is foreshadowed in the baptism of Jesus by John the Baptist in the River Jordan, as early Christians were well aware. Despite claims made by various scholars, there is very little evidence that early Christians were terribly embarrassed that Jesus had been baptized by John. Rather, as indications in the Gospels suggest, along with more explicit interpretations of the event by the Church Fathers, Christians saw in the baptism of the Lord the mystery of both incarnation and incorporation. In other words, in this significant event — which would eventually gain the title of "Theophany" ("Manifestation of God") — the basic outline of salvation was thought to be provided in miniature.

As the tradition and the New Testament present it, when Christ is baptized, the Father acclaims him and the Spirit descends and remains upon him. God is thereby revealed, and Jesus is shown to be the one through whom the gift of the Holy Spirit — synonymous with the gift of eternal life — comes into the world.

As he descends to the banks of the Jordan, rubbing shoulders with those who have come to confess their sins, repent, and be forgiven, Jesus is designated by John the Baptist to be "the Lamb of God, who takes away the sins of the world" (John 1:29). He is the one who will carry upon himself, like the scapegoat in the Old Testament (cf. Lev. 16), the sins of the whole world into the wilderness of death itself, only to rise again with the promise of immortality. In Matthew's account, the Baptist, recognizing Jesus as the one whose coming he was sent to announce, is depicted as uncomfortable with Christ's presenting himself for baptism. In response to John's expostulation — "I need to be baptized by you, and do you come to me?" — Jesus replies, "Let it be so now; for thus it is fitting for us to fulfill all righteousness" (Matt. 3:14-15). What this means is that what Jesus does at his baptism is not for his own sake, but rather for the church he will establish

(Matt. 16:18; 28:19-20). He *fulfills* all righteousness on his disciples' behalf. Or, as Paul put it, "But now the righteousness of God has been manifested apart from law, although the law and the prophets bear witness to it, the righteousness of God through faith in Jesus Christ for all who believe" (Rom. 3:21-22).

The Church Fathers, and the Eastern tradition especially, saw in Christ's descent into the Jordan the cleansing of the waters of the world: he purified them for the sacrament of Christian baptism. Their incarnational insight was that God does not bypass material creation to come to us. Indeed, the Incarnation consecrates material creation, preparing it for its ultimate transformation in the risen Christ (cf. Rom. 8:18-25). Even more, our own incorporation into Christ's body through baptism affects us, annihilating our sins in the death and burial of Jesus, and causing us here and now to share ontologically in the indestructible life of the ascended Lord.

Of all this, Christ's own baptism was viewed as a sign and a revelation. In a mystical sense he was immersed incarnationally in our humanity, and through the incorporation of our baptism we are sacramentally immersed in his divinity. Baptism is, then, both an inseparable *union* with Christ, and — in Christ — an inseparable *union* with all other baptized disciples everywhere. We need to hold on to that theme of union — unity — as we turn our attention now to the other great Gospel sacrament, that of communion or the Eucharist.

It is impossible to appreciate the meaning and purpose of communion in the life of the church without some rudimentary knowledge of the interrelationship of covenant, sacrifice, and mutual participation in a meal in ancient Middle Eastern and Jewish culture. If anything should remind Christians that their religion is eastern Mediterranean in origin and that they are spiritually related to the mother faith of Judaism, spiritual descendants and heirs of Abraham, it is the sacrament of the Eucharist (cf. Rom. 4:16; 11:13-24). After centuries of distinctively non-Semitic Christian liturgies, the Jewish character of the Eucharist has been obscured, and the vital covenantal significance of it too often forgotten. On the one hand, the meaning is lost when the Eucharist is perceived as a "private" matter between the communicant and God alone, as if the communal aspect has little bearing on the individual's "pious reception" of the "sacred species" (a ghastly phrase if ever there was one). On the other hand, neither is communion simply a "celebration" of "togetherness"; it is nothing less than the seal of personal loyalty, the solemn recommitment of oneself to personal discipleship in a binding covenant with the whole, catholic community of Christ's disciples.

At its most basic, the Christian Eucharist is a "meal," a banquet. In a Middle Eastern context, this in itself is significant. Mutual meal-sharing, involving in these cultures even a sharing from the same dishes, is a sign of fellowship and unity. Those who eat together are bound together on some level of commitment to one another. In traditional Middle Eastern culture, meals mean something more than refueling; they imply and often ensure relationship of a binding nature. So it is that there can be nothing conceivably more loathsome than an act of betrayal perpetrated by someone with whom one has shared his table. One is reminded of this, for example, by the words of Psalm 41:9 (quoted in John 13:18 in reference to Judas): "Even my bosom friend in whom I trusted, who ate of my bread, has lifted his heel against me." The emphasis in this verse is not just on the unconscionable act of betrayal itself — that would have been despicable enough; it is on the fact that the betrayal is compounded by a former sharing of bread between the betrayer and the betrayed. Betrayal after breaking bread together — that's as low as it gets.

In the Old Testament, a covenantal agreement between two

parties is sealed by sacrifice and a sacrificial meal. To choose a single example, one can look at the covenant established between those two consummate con artists, Jacob and his Uncle Laban (Gen. 31). When Jacob fled from the latter and was overtaken, the two men settled their differences by "cutting a covenant" with one another. Laban suggested that an agreement be struck: "Come now, let us make a covenant, you and I; and let it be a witness between you and me" (Gen. 31:44). The terms having been made, Laban then underscored the weightiness of any breach of the contract: "The LORD watch between you and me, when we are absent one from another" (Gen. 31:49). This, it should be noted, is not a greeting-card sentiment. It is, in fact, a grave warning with an implicit threat attached. It means that God will judge severely the one who violates the covenant: "See this heap [of stones] and the pillar, which I have set [as a boundary marker] between you and me. This heap is a witness, and the pillar is a witness, that I will not pass over this heap to you, and you will not pass over this heap and this pillar to me, for harm . . ." (Gen. 31:51-52). After this pronouncement, the covenant between them was "cut" — that is to say, an animal was slain. This action meant that, if either party broke the terms of the covenant, the violator could likewise expect to be slain. Afterward, the sacrificial meal was eaten, shared by both parties: "Jacob offered a sacrifice on the mountain and called his kinsmen [Laban and those with him] to eat bread" (Gen. 31:54).

In this text we see a basic outline of Middle Eastern covenant-making, with its features of sacrifice and sacrificial meal. It is essentially the same "shape" found in the establishing of the covenant between God and the Israelite "assembly" (in Hebrew, *qahal;* in Greek, *ekklesia,* or "church") in Exodus 24. At the foot of Mount Sinai, Moses offers sacrifice, using the blood, the symbol of life itself, to consecrate the altar and the people. The covenant agreement is made on the terms that God has privileged Israel with his Law, and they will in turn endeavor to live accordingly — leading holy lives in company with the holy God in their midst:

> Then [Moses] took the book of the covenant, and read it in the hearing of the people; and they said, "All that the LORD has spoken we will do, and we will be obedient." And Moses took the blood and threw it upon the people, and said, "Behold the blood of the covenant which the LORD has made with you in accordance with all these words." (Exod. 24:7-8)

This is followed by a covenant meal on Mount Sinai, with the chief men of Israel accompanying Moses for the extraordinary encounter: "They beheld God, and ate and drank" (Exod. 24:11).

It is, correspondingly, the identical outline that shapes the Christian Eucharist, in which Christ presents "the blood of the New Covenant." Christ is himself the mediator (like Moses) in this case, and also the one with whom the covenant is made (as was God in the Exodus account), and also the sacrifice (like the bulls of sacrifice, whose blood was sprinkled on the people). He provides, as well, for the sake of his body the church, in which we are baptized, the sacrificial meal and sustenance of the "assembly." Through the mystery of this sacrament, the bread and wine convey to those who receive them the sacrificial "body and blood," or, to use the even more obviously sacrificial language of John's Gospel, the "flesh and blood" of Christ, "divided" in sacrifice by the "cutting" of the New Covenant (1 Cor. 10:16-17; John 6:51-58). That this was intended to be taken as indeed the incarnate Christ's sacrificed body and blood went undoubted for many centuries in the history of the church. It needed no explanation or detailed definitions. It required only faith that — "in Christ" — the body received him and his covenant anew in every celebration of the sacrament. That this one sacrifice, completed once and for all on the cross, could be extended and made accessible in all places under the sun by the risen and ascended Lord was likewise accepted by all believers. What mattered above all were the covenant and the unity with Christ and one another that the sacrament effected.

It is Paul's account of the institution of the Eucharist that puts before us the gravity of the sacrament's covenantal force in the early church. After warning the Corinthian Christians that they could not be partakers *(koinonoi)* in the table of the Lord's body and blood and also be partakers in pagan temple feasts (1 Cor. 10:16-17, 21), which would constitute in effect a violation of covenant conditions, he turns his attention in 1 Corinthians 11 to the matter of disharmony among believers who were receiving communion together.

Here he addresses with tough words the seriousness of violating the covenant meal. He alludes, in fact, to the act of betrayal of Jesus by Judas, who had, like them, also partaken of the Lord's Supper: "For I received from the Lord what I also delivered to you, that the Lord Jesus *on the night when he was betrayed* took bread . . ." (1 Cor. 11:23; emphasis mine). This phrase has passed on into most Eucharistic liturgies and is barely noticed as a result. It is, though, important to remember that Paul is not here writing a liturgical text when he describes that particular night as that of the *betrayal* of the Lord — he is making a point. The point is that Judas violated the covenant immediately after his participation in the covenant meal. A more heinous act than that could not be conceived. This is why Paul could later say, following the Greek text, "Whoever, therefore, eats the bread or drinks the cup of the Lord in an unworthy manner *will be guilty of profaning the body and blood of the Lord* [i.e., guilty of his death]. . . . For any one who eats and drinks without discerning the body eats and drinks judgment upon himself" (1 Cor. 11:27, 29; emphasis mine).

Paul's meaning would have been sharp and clear to his readers. To be "guilty of profaning the body and blood of the Lord" is nothing less than to betray him — indeed, to be responsible for his crucifixion. It is, in a way, to repeat the act of Judas. In Corinth, the inability to "discern the body" meant an inability to recognize that one is in covenant with all who share in the body of Christ. Paul presumably means by "body" here both the sacrament and that which participation in the sacrament signifies: the unity of the church through the disciples' covenanted commitment. In 1 Corinthians 12 he would go on to write at length about the church as the body, and in Chapter 10 he had already stressed that communion creates that body: "Because there is one bread, we who are many are one body, for we all partake of the one bread" (1 Cor. 10:17).

The Corinthian Christians failed to realize that, whenever they gathered together to eat the sacred meal, they were renewing their baptismal covenant with both Christ and his whole church. They were binding themselves in Christ one to another. To mistreat each other, to gossip about each another, to create divisions between rich and poor (the chief sin in Corinth related to the sacrament), to break the moral laws established by God, and so on, was to violate the covenant. It was, in effect, to repeat the action of Judas, becoming "guilty of profaning the body and blood of the Lord." In so doing, says Paul, one receives "judgment" instead of covenantal grace. Indeed, he indicates, it is the same Christ who is received in the sacrament, but he can be received either as savior or as judge. It is the nature of the covenant that establishes both possibilities. (To use the later language of sacramental theology, the efficacy of the sacrament depends on the disposition of the one receiving it.)

However, Paul, as ever, emphasizes grace, not judgment. "Let a man examine himself," he writes, "and so eat of the bread and drink of the cup" (1 Cor. 11:28). In other words, the Lord wants you at his table — his desire is that you take your rightful places and together, as one body, receive at his hands the life he offers. "If we judged ourselves truly," Paul writes encouragingly, "we should not be judged" (1 Cor. 11:31). Paul is clear that this is a sacrament of grace — a freely bestowed covenant of redemption and healing. This is expressed in the second of three Eucharistic exhortations (introduced in 1552) in *The Book of Common Prayer,* designed to be read aloud to Anglican congregations by their parish priests: "In God's behalf, I bid you all that are here present; and beseech you, for the Lord Jesus Christ's sake, that ye will not refuse to come thereto, being so lovingly called and bidden by God himself. . . . I exhort you, as ye love your own salvation, that ye will be partakers of this holy communion."

One of the finest poems of George Herbert, which appears at the beginning of this chapter, was probably inspired by this exhortation in the English Prayer Book, and it articulates movingly the same gracious summons of the Lord to his people to join him at the table. Judgment is not the last word, but grace, and — with it — the ongoing invitation to all disciples to participate and to maintain unity between themselves. There is to be sacramental unity, and no sacramental "walls."

II.

From the cursory overviews of baptism and communion above, then, four key words emerge: incarnation, incorporation, covenant, and unity. Christ comes by his incarnation to humanity and all creation (for example, by his baptism, "cleansing the waters"), taking part in it and uniting it to the divine indissolubly. He draws so close that he even assumes our sins and carries them from us, inviting us into the covenant he establishes. We in turn come to Christ and are baptized — that is to say, "immersed" — in him, and, becoming members of his body, we are resurrected sacramentally and ascended with him. This is incorporation. Again, this is also essentially what it means for us to respond to his invitation and enter into the covenant with him and with one another, ratified by the sacrifice of his body and blood. This covenant is reconfirmed whenever we "eat this bread and drink the cup" in communion, and thus "proclaim the Lord's death until he comes" (1 Cor. 11:26). These sacraments, these "outward and visible signs" of incarnation, incorporation, and covenant, establish the grounds of our unity in Christ, the *koinonia* we share. *And unity is where we begin, not something for which we should be required to hope.*

This is a crucial point, and one that has been obscured by millennia of church divisiveness, which — ironically enough — has been one of the chief consequences of Christendom for Christianity. That there was disunity in the church during the first two and a half centuries is beyond doubt. But, during those more loosely governed centuries, the leaders of the church could appeal to those in disunity to remember their common baptism and spiritual union in the sacraments, and not to deny their bonds of charity in Christ.

One can hear such an appeal, perhaps, in the words of 1 John 2:19: "They went out from us, but they were not of us; for if they had been of us, they would have continued with us; but they went out, that it might be plain that they all are not of us." We have no idea, really, who it is who "went out," but it seems quite feasible that, whoever they were, they could come back if and when they chose. The door wasn't locked and bolted against them. Clearly, their refusal to "continue" in fellowship was their own doing, and the writer of the letter doesn't approve.

Of course, there are bitter moments even in the pages of the New Testament: Paul's anger at what he perceives as a false gospel (see, for instance, and most strikingly, Gal. 5:12); a case of excommunication for sexual immorality (1 Cor. 5; but see the later 2 Cor. 2:5-11, which *may* refer to the same situation; regarding excommunication, see also Matt. 18:15-20); and the book of Revelation's fierce denunciations of the apparently libertine "Nicolaitans" and a Christian prophetess and her followers (Rev. 2:14-16, 20-25). Life in the early church was hardly a bed of roses, and division was certainly not uncommon even then, human nature being what it is.

Still, the assumption was that, gross sins apart, Christians were united in the covenant, and so — whatever differences might arise to create division — all should realize their essential unity in Christ and seek to maintain it. Even when Paul was faced with the problems surrounding the Eucharist in the church of Corinth, as touched upon above, it was a sin *against* charity and unity that provoked him to refer to their actions as a betrayal of Christ. It was not a sin of false doctrine, but a sin of false love. As we saw, his conclusion was not one of unremitting judgment, but an exhortation to get right and receive the sacrament together in a proper state. Here he pronounces no anathemas (and even when he pronounces anathemas in another place, it is a matter of anger regarding a threat from outside to his churches' internal unity; Gal. 1:8-9). In other words, it was an appeal to their ontological unity as the very basis for their need to be reconciled and restored. Baptized and one body in Christ, in covenant and community, they had every incentive to hold themselves together without fracturing.

It is, in light of the above, significant to note that the first great patristic defender of orthodoxy in the early church — early enough to be just one generational step from the apostles themselves — described heretics as those who departed from the apostolic and orthodox churches of their own accord to found their separated churches. I mean, of course, the great Irenaeus of Lyons, who wrote his masterpiece, *Against the Heresies,* between 175 and 185. In other words, heretics were not those "thrown out" by tyrannical bishops, but those who broke fellowship and communion, and invented their own alternative dogmas. There is no reason to doubt that Irenaeus's view of these early heretics is correct. The early orthodox and catholic church, as we saw in the last chapter, was inclusive and embracing of a wide range of perspectives, as demonstrated by the breadth of the New Testament canon. Heretics were those who were not content to accept even this wideness of accepted belief, but insisted on taking themselves and others outside the *regula fidei* itself. They chose to violate their sacramental covenant bond.[1]

Down to the present day we see in those surviving churches with a Semitic heritage, like the (Nestorian) Assyrian Church of the East, with its Syriac liturgy (Syriac being, in essence, the same language that Jesus spoke — i.e., Aramaic), the living belief that all churches with apostolic origin — despite even serious doctrinal rifts — are already one in baptism and should naturally share together in communion. Their practice, unchanged for two thousand years and reflective of the original Christian mind, has been to keep an "open" communion between themselves and all those who are baptized and profess Christ, across ecclesiastical lines. There is no such thing in their practice as "impaired communion" or non-sharing in the sacrament with fellow believers whose churches profess the apostolic tradition. For them, quite

1. See, for example, Irenaeus of Lyons, *Against the Heresies,* Bk. V, 20, 1-2.

rightly, all believers are viewed as entitled to share in communion (which is *Christ's* table, and not the property of any institution or hierarchy). Communion is understood as the Pentecostal fire that *creates* unity between Christians. Participation in it is not based on full agreement with an institution's every doctrinal stance, assuming the apostolic basics are adhered to as fundamental. One *begins* by affirming union with Christ and other believers *before* dealing with whatever doctrinal differences may exist. The Church of the East, then, seeing in the Eucharist the divine fire, recognizes an inherent transforming power in the sacrament. Ecclesial unity cannot simply depend on the churches' full agreement, but must rely on their communion with Christ — *which is already present.* Jesus' prayer "that they all may be one" in John 17 is seen as directly related to the shared food of everlasting life in John 6. The ancient — possibly first-century — text, the *Didache* (IX, 4), exhorted Christians to pray at the Eucharist that the scattered children of God be drawn, like so many grains of wheat, into one loaf, one church and Christ's body.

Incarnation, incorporation, and covenant are not directly affected by doctrinal discord; rather, doctrinal discord has a chance of being worked out if unity in these fundamental truths is assumed from the beginning. People who share the covenant meal are bound together, these churches assume, and therefore they have a chance of restoring, like a family, whatever else may be wrong between them. This was likewise the New Testament ideal — and, indeed, it is a Semitic ideal. Those few Christian bodies that have preserved these deepest of Christian roots have kept alive also this truest vision of sacramental unity.

So, what happened with those other churches — those whose roots were less Semitic, which theologized and liturgized in philosophical Greek and legalese-inclined Latin, and eventually in a plethora of other languages as well, instead of earthy, poetic

Aramaic? What happened that led to their cracking up and splintering into thousands of bits? Succinctly put, what happened was Christendom.

The Oriental churches, such as the Assyrian Church of the East, fell outside the influence of imperial Roman and Constantinopolitan Christendom after the fourth century. They were in the East, after all, the Middle East and even further east over time, and the rest of the churches — even what we think of as "Eastern" Orthodoxy — were churches of the West. With Christendom, Greek and Latin supplant Syriac, and the empire dictates what is to unify the imperial church — and what unifies it is to be dogma and orthodoxy, thus hardening into adamantine weapons these good and necessary aspects of Christianity and using them, often quite literally, against flesh and blood. It is the beginning of dogmatism, and dogmatic "unity" dethrones sacramental unity. The imperial church's desire for doctrinal unity ironically contributes to the fracturing of the body, and, with the first execution of heretics in 385, the church of the West starts down an ignominious path. To preserve "unity," people are "cut off" and even cut down and cut to pieces.

In time, the East will be divided between Byzantine Orthodoxy, Nestorianism, and Monophysitism (etc., etc.); the West will divide itself from the East; Protestant will divide from Catholic; Protestant will divide from Protestant. . . . And the issue will always be "doctrinal purity" and unity rooted in right belief — or else no unity at all. Wars will be fought, people tortured and burned, iconoclasm and destruction visited by one type of Christian upon another's sacred spaces; and all the time dogmas will, in the hands of theologians and approved by "authorities," become more and more abstruse and perplexing to the common baptized man and woman. Communion itself will become a key battleground: Is Christ *really present*? *How* is he "really present"? Should the bread be leavened or unleavened? Is the Mass a sacrifice or a shared meal only? Is it a memorial? Is it transubstantiation, consubstantiation, receptionism . . . ? Is Christ's body and blood spiritually or corporeally received? And so on and so on. One can only wonder what the apostles would have thought of all this, or how much of it they even would have understood, because — truth be told — none of these issues would probably have made sense in a Semitic context. It was enough to know that Christ was really present in their midst, communicating himself to them anew as they once again reaffirmed the unifying covenant in his body and blood.

Christendom, with its zeal for uniformity over unity, thus distorted Christianity and divided Christians. When we look about us, in the wake of Christendom, we see a chaos of dogmatized and denominationalized versions of Christianity. Denominations are remnants of this rending: all of them in one way or another — either by insistence on their own doctrinal purity over against their doctrinal rivals, or by their own distinctive historical investments in the innumerable battles of the past — attest to the invasive ravages of Christendom's principles throughout Europe and elsewhere upon the sacramental unity of Christianity.

Where do we begin to put right this monumental mess?

I believe the answers are simple, but implementation of them will mean going down a long, bumpy road, with countless reinforced barriers along the way. So, here are my simple answers, which I share as suggestions.

The first thing to keep in mind is that, as Christendom wanes, we are under no national, doctrinal, or divine obligation to adhere exclusively to any one institutional expression of the church. Antiquity may rightly be an incentive to be a Roman Catholic, Orthodox, or Oriental Christian; or one's preference or theological leanings or birthright might keep one contentedly in, say, the Anglican or Baptist or Methodist churches. I, for one, would not wish to be in a non-liturgical church, and I'm as thoroughly High-Church Anglican in my sensibilities as I can be. Still, being a Christian is vital; being an Anglican is not. Likewise, accessibility to one's preferred communion or denomination may be prevented by distance or some other factor. Let that person find a congregation of whatever kind is readily available, one that suits him or her, whether it meets in a church building or a friend's living room or is a storefront church, and, recalling always that no church is perfect, seek to grow in Christ there. In the spirit of the Pauline beatitude, "Happy is he who has no reason to judge himself for what he approves" (Rom. 14:22).

But one should also not be expected to maintain old patterns of institutional divisiveness. Paul also warns, "Let us then pursue what makes for peace and mutual upbuilding" (Rom. 14:19). "For the kingdom of God is not," he writes, "food and drink [meaning, in this context, matters of ceremonial legality] but righteousness and peace and joy in the Holy Spirit; he who thus serves Christ is acceptable to God and approved by men" (Rom. 14:17-18). In creedal dogma (see Chapter Two above), one should find sufficient agreed beliefs to bind one to all other orthodox believers, whatever their ecclesial home might be; but in more subtle and detailed teaching one should not seek grounds for unity. Unity is the basis for doctrinal refinement and even internal debate; those more elaborate and not clearly basic (creedal) doctrines, along with all institutional barriers created to defend them, should not be regarded as the basis for unity. These should be ignored when the sacrament of unity is offered. It is the refusal to break covenant that holds the church together even in the face of doctrinal disagreements. Covenantal charity precedes all else in the body of Christ.

This, in turn, means that we overlook barriers and walls as

best we can. No altar or communion table is barred to us by Christ, because the sacraments belong to Christ. By his incarnation, he has drawn near to us and gathered us. He alone offers the invitation to his church. By our incorporation in him, we are already one body with him and with one another. There is no reason why we should not come to the table of the Lord, assuming that a church's beliefs are essentially apostolic (in accord with the *regula fidei,* as discussed above in Chapter Two), and assuming that we are baptized disciples of Jesus. For the sake of others' sensibilities, we may find that we should refrain from partaking ("Everything is indeed clean, but it is wrong for any one to make others fall by what he eats"; Rom. 14:20). Charity for others, whose faith may be weaker than our own, is always the guiding rule for our conduct in any such situation ("it is right not to eat meat or drink wine or do anything that makes your brother stumble . . ."; "let each of us please his neighbor for his good . . ."; Rom. 14:21; 15:2). But that should be the only consideration, apart from concern for keeping to apostolic essentials. Neither historical splits, nor the peculiar dogmas of this or that institution, nor hierarchical decrees, nor forbidding authorities — none of these are true barriers to Christ's sacrament. He says, "Take, eat; this is my body. . . . Drink of it [the cup], all of you; for this is my blood of the covenant" (Matt. 26:26, 27-28). On this, Christ is insistent, as George Herbert's poem underscores: " 'You must sit down,' says Love, 'and taste my meat.'/So I did sit and eat."

As I said, the way is long and bumpy, and such freedom of action as I propose will be hindered by, and unacceptable to, many who see themselves as defenders of the faith and doorkeepers to Christ's sacraments in their various churches. Open communion is practiced by some, but closed communion is the norm in many churches as well. The time has come, I believe, to act as if there is no closed communion, because, in fact, in Christ, for Christians, there really is no such thing. It is the illusion of Christendom that has made it seem so, along with the idea that dogmatism trumps charity and that doctrinal purity — that ultimately impossible achievement — is more to be desired than Christ's own open invitation.

Incarnation, incorporation, covenant, and unity. These four are ontologically our home, our being and hope, where we dwell, and who we are. The sacraments express this basic, essential, indissoluble reality. Divisions exist only in our collective mind, the remnants of an old order, derived from the Constantinian *imperium* and not from Jesus' *ekklesia*. The way to unity is to root ourselves once more in our own identity, as baptized in Christ's eternally undivided body, and to ignore the massive illusions of disunity. We must try to begin to recover an even older order. That older order, older than Christendom and its destructive mania for uniformity, is the order of covenant loyalty. The real sin is to break it, which — as Paul said — is betrayal and akin to the act of Judas.

One of our most rebellious actions — ignoring institutional barriers to sacramental unity — could just possibly be the most genuine and radical act of obedience to Jesus in a post-Christendom world.

FIVE

SAYING YES TO EVANGELISM, AND NO TO POLEMICISM

And Jesus came and said to them, "All authority in heaven and on earth has been given to me. Go therefore and make disciples of all nations, baptizing them in the name of the Father and of the Son and of the Holy Spirit, teaching them to observe all that I have commanded you; and lo, I am with you always, to the close of the age."

Matthew 28:18-20

I.

In a time when we see all too plainly the unattractive aspects of the churches in the media, we can be tempted to question even the basic truths upon which Christian discipleship is founded. After all, haven't the churches failed? Consider these examples.

When we look at the Roman Catholic Church, we find a church whose moral authority has become seriously eroded, and — sadly — deservedly so. How it will recover after thousands of cases of child and youth rape by clergy on an international scale, its hierarchy complicit in covering up the scandals for decades until the very proliferation of the disease among its ranks could no longer be hidden, remains to be seen. There has never before been a time when this once great, at times exquisitely beautiful, embodiment of imperial Christianity has sunk to such depths as it has today. Not even the fabled decadence of the Borgias rivals it. It is a tragedy of monumental proportions, repulsive to any morally attuned mind; and its demoralizing consequences may be, in some future age, measured in centuries and not merely in years.

Turning to evangelical Christianity in the United States and elsewhere, we find that this version of Protestantism has far too often given itself over to an anti-intellectual message of materialism, success, neo-conservative values, unbridled capitalism, and political power-brokering. Scientism may be a problem on the one hand in our secular culture (as noted in Chapter One), poking the scientific nose into areas of life where it has no credentials, authority, or say; but fundamentalism's fight against irrefutable science is a glaring intellectual scandal of the first order. Disappointingly, as well, evangelicals are frequently at the forefront of America's most bloodthirsty segment of the general population, supporting the so-called War on Terror, the torture of suspects, and hard-line police tactics; it is given too easily to the uncritical confusion of Christianity with a raw American militaristic triumphalism of the most aggressive kind.

Mainline ("liberal") Protestantism, meantime, continues to evaporate like an insubstantial morning mist. Left-wing in politics, "nice," bland, ineffective, graying, vague in message, spineless in matters of sexual morality, and doctrinally vaporous, it has little spark left within it and suffers from a relentless loss of numbers from its pews.

And so on. The handwriting might well seem to be on the wall — "weighed and found wanting."

There are, of course, healthy renewals and revivals in all the major ecclesiastical bodies — Catholic, Orthodox, Anglican, and Protestant — for which we may be thankful. But even these churches are finding it difficult to contend with the crass and coarse toxins flowing through a secularized materialist culture, one dominated by media that are on average execrable. The fastest-growing "faith" at the present time among youth is a dumbed-down, sneering, arrogant and uninformed pop version of "atheism" — meaning, in fact, anti-religiousness — and this misnamed fundamentalist "atheism" in turn has come to be increasingly identified with secularism. It's a tough struggle for intelligent Christian disciples to face such a flood of crude ignorance and boorish propaganda.

One might indeed, then, be tempted to think that the churches have failed, but that's only part of the story. They have also survived and been a voice at times against the flood of secular evils and the worst materialist tyrannies of the last century. With the rise of secularism, the world saw its worst genocides and most monstrous and devastating wars. After the twentieth century, one would think that no sane human being could ever have a high opinion of secularism or scientism again; that these — most glaringly in the forms of fascism and Communism — had shown themselves to be frauds and morally repellent.

Meanwhile, Christians find themselves in a reactionary position. Despite the failures of institutions, however, which are mostly the failures of bureaucracies and hierarchies to act in ways reflective of Christ's kingdom, I believe that Christians should not permit themselves to fall into reactionary behaviors. They should resist any temptations to claim victimization and whining on the one hand, and, on the other, to become feisty and cantankerous. And one significantly reactionary temptation, among more intellectually gifted orthodox Christians, is to engage in sharp-edged polemics — often justified as "apologetics" or "defending" the faith — with those who "challenge the faith." I say this is a temptation, not a virtue.

117

The purpose of apologetics, as popularly understood, is to present "evidence," as best one can, of the truth of the gospel. Evidence for the existence of God, evidence of Christ's divinity, evidence of his resurrection from the dead, and so on, is considered essential for meeting the cultured despisers of the faith on their own turf. But, as I will argue in this final chapter, this is not what Christians are primarily called to do, even if occasionally allowances can be made for dignified debate with unbelievers. In an age when so much in the churches requires renewal and reformation, any debate with unbelievers is something that should be — at the very least — handled with great care, exhibiting no arrogance and much humility.

The verse of Scripture most often used to support polemical "apologetics" is 1 Peter 3:15: "Always be prepared to make a defense [*apologian*] to any one who calls you to account for the hope that is in you, yet do it with gentleness and reverence. . . ." Nonetheless, we need to observe closely the original context of this statement. If one reads it with the full passage in mind, one finds that the word *apologia* is used in its classical Greek legal sense, and thus it has very little to do with polemics or the presentation of "evidence." Rather, it refers to the response one gives in a situation where one has been charged with something possibly criminal in nature. Verse 14 refers to suffering "for righteousness' sake." "Have no fear of them," the text exhorts, presumably referring to those presenting charges or making accusations, "nor be troubled. . . ." Verses 16-18, which follow the text in question, continue the line of thought: "Keep your conscience clear, so that, when you are abused, those who revile your good behavior in Christ may be put to shame. For it is better to suffer for doing right, if that should be God's will, than for doing wrong. For Christ also died. . . ." In this context, 1 Peter 3:15 clearly has to do with accusation, charges leveled, condemnation, and the

118

proper conduct of Christians when thus persecuted. It has to do with "suffering" for "doing right," as Christ also suffered. The "defense" in question — meaning here a reasoned response — is not to present "evidence" of one's doctrinal theories, but to give a "gentle and reverent" rationale for why Christians do what they do and live as they live.

The assumption in this passage is that, if a Christian lives the sort of kingdom ideals that Christ taught, he or she should be prepared to be considered non-Roman, unpatriotic, a troublemaker, an outcast, a potential threat, and someone whose Lord — executed with a slave's death for claiming to be a "king" within Caesar's domain — is manifestly not the same "lord" as the empire's. The issue here isn't at all about giving "evidential" argumentation about, say, God's existence or Christ's resurrection — such things were meant to be simply proclaimed as "good news" from God (a point to which we shall return). Rather, this verse is an exhortation to tell an interrogator or magistrate why Christians live "righteously," and not as others do — why, for example, they do not make offerings to the emperor's "genius," or why they eschew roles of public service (such as the military), or why they are "atheists" (which, in this context, meant those who failed to worship the gods as Rome prescribed, with the expected sacrifices), or why some of their women chose to reject their families' expectations concerning betrothals, or why their gatherings were held in secret and their "mysteries" undisclosed. It's a defense of Christian ethics and the Christian way of life, and not at all a matter of doctrinal polemics. And, most importantly, because it is a matter of defending a loving, peaceful, nonviolent, and forgiving way of life, the disciple must manifestly be that kind of person in his or her behavior. It is a defense not of theory, but of practice — though certainly practice that is rooted in theory. What theory? A theory stated in simple terms in early creedal assertions such as these: "For us there is one God, the Father, from whom are all things and for whom we exist, and one Lord, Jesus Christ, through whom are all things and through whom we exist"; "Jesus is Lord"; "Christ died for our sins in accordance with the scriptures, . . . he was buried, . . . he was raised on the third day in accordance with the scriptures"; and "We must all appear before the judgment seat of Christ" (1 Cor. 8:6, 12:3, 15:3-4; 2 Cor. 5:10).

These are plain statements of faith. We Christians believe them to be at the heart of what we proclaim and the motivation for the lives we lead. We don't need to present "evidence" for their credibility on grounds laid out by others. There is no "evidence" that others can present that show these beliefs to be either untrue or unwise. Christianity isn't just a "head trip" or a string of theoretical "truth claims." The only decisive evidence before non-Christians for the credibility of our beliefs is what is exhibited in our lives. And that's the most difficult thing for us to face — that the earnestness of our faith is solely a matter of our pragmatic attempts to apply the teachings of Christ to ourselves. Our "answer" to the world should first be a response to the question, whether spoken or unspoken, "What is it you *do?*" and *not* "What is it you say you believe?" Arguments will impress no one if they are only arguments about our doctrinal assertions.

It was the late Carl Sagan, the pre-eminent science popularizer, who made the oft-quoted statement, aimed at religious believers, that "extraordinary claims require extraordinary evidence." And, sad to say, Christians have often felt intimidated by that seeming bit of wisdom for three decades. It has been repeated so frequently by atheists, anti-religionists, and pushers of scientism that we almost have bought the notion ourselves, and we have apologists who spend a great deal of energy in debates with prominent pop-atheists, providing as much "evidence" as possible. If we stop to consider this for a moment, we should recognize what a tar-baby situation this is. There could never be enough "evidence" to satisfy the convinced anti-religionist. The more we jab at him, the more tangled up in his mental mess we find ourselves, and, when the bell rings or the time is up, and we extricate ourselves from the "debate," we know that, invariably, we will just have to debate the same topics all over again at the next "debate." It's an endless sport for some. Nothing can be proved when we put ourselves on the anti-religionists' turf. The game is rigged from the outset. All it has accomplished is a monumental waste of perfectly good time.

The scientistic materialist "requires" evidence — indeed, he requires "extraordinary" evidence — and we go trotting out onto his playing field, right along with his terms and rules of engagement, trying to meet his endless demands. We score a hit, a very palpable hit, perhaps, and yet it's not enough. For every thrust and parry, there is a cut and sidestep from the other. It never ends. It can't end. Arguing, polemics, debate — these are insufficient and a distraction from discipleship and growth in wisdom. That's not an evasion; it's a simple fact. We sometimes forget that, precisely because we are meant to be cultivating "a pure heart," we are to "have nothing to do with stupid, senseless controversies," because "they breed quarrels," and "the Lord's servant must not be quarrelsome" (2 Tim. 2:22-24). "As for the man who is weak in faith," says Paul, "welcome him, but not for disputes over opinions" (Rom. 14:1). When it comes to hot debates, apologetics, and polemics with despisers of faith, we should be none too eager to involve ourselves.

Besides, we really are not "required" to supply evidence, let alone "extraordinary" evidence, to anybody. First, we should ask ourselves who it is that claims to "require" such a thing of us. I will go so far as to say that, even if the question were about belief in the existence of elves and goblins, we should rather prefer to have a society that allows us the wild and unhindered freedom to believe in such things, than one in which those who lack anything like a normal imagination forbid us that basic human right. It is not for bureaucratic, micro-managing social engineers to interfere with the beliefs or dreams or hopes of human beings.

But, moving from trivial and harmless (maybe crazy) fancies to genuine articles of serious belief, ones bolstered by intellectual integrity and the full range of perennial human sensibilities, we should even more adamantly resist any outside pressure to narrow our selves and our spiritual lives to the pinched confines of the materialistic anti-religionists' mental universe. So, who is it that "requires" us to provide extraordinary evidence? An atheist demanding "evidence" for God's existence, perhaps, or a promoter of the scientistic agenda demanding "evidence" of Christ's resurrection? In what sense are we *required* to satisfy such demands? To say it straight, we don't owe evidence to anyone who demands it of us. Jesus told us in no uncertain terms how to treat the sneering and boorish: "Do not give dogs what is holy; and do not throw your pearls before swine, lest they trample them under foot and turn to attack you" (Matt. 7:6). This is neither his most-quoted command nor his nicest phraseology (Jesus nowhere obliges us to "be nice," but only not to be abusive and violent); but it packs a wallop and we should listen to it. Jesus is telling us to walk away and evade "stupid, senseless controversies" — silence is a sign of wisdom in the face of foolishness. It is dignified, and it doesn't sink to a low level. Nor is Jesus condemning or insulting individual persons with his analogies of "dogs" and "swine," but a specific attitude of mind that lacks respect for what it doesn't appreciate. The contemptuous should receive stony silence and a turned back from us, not explanation or recrimination or a sign of undignified weakness. Simply silence, a drawn curtain, and a refusal to argue. If they alter their behavior and show genuine interest, we continue the discussion. Otherwise, we drop it.

The "requirement" for "extraordinary" evidence is an absurdity in itself, and should be regarded as such. What can "extraordinary" even mean where "evidence" is concerned? Surely, belief in God is not in itself an "extraordinary" phenomenon among human beings, so to claim such a belief is justifiable in itself. No apologetic is necessary. (And, if one is pressed to "define" God, the only polite response is to say, as kindly and gently as one can manage, that no one can "define" God. "In him we live, move, and have our being"; it's not the other way around.) Either one believes in God, or a transcendent order of being, or one does not. The majority of humankind has believed in it, in one form or another, since time immemorial. An "extraordinary" assertion it is not. And even if one can say, for example, that Jesus' resurrection is an "extraordinary claim," it still is a claim about a singular event that, for rather obvious reasons, cannot be reproduced. It can no more be reproduced than any other event in the historical record. Unlike scientists in a laboratory, historians must often settle for only documentary evidence. The testimonies to Christ's resurrection are documentary evidence, and the evidence is copious, to say the least. It is, by precise definition, "ordinary" evidence, of course; but then there really is no such thing as *extraordinary* evidence. That's a red herring. The very demand is meaningless, and should be treated as such. Again, either one accepts or one rejects the claims regarding Jesus' resurrection; but we should not entertain any unreasonable demand for impossible "extraordinary evidence." Either the evidence (*any* kind of evidence, including scientific) is "ordinary," or it cannot exist at all. There can only be "ordinary" — not "extraordinary" — evidence for anything.

If that isn't enough, we also find that there are "mythicists" on the loose, riding the ranges of the blogosphere and the loonier halls of academe, and denying that Jesus ever existed (and now Muhammad, too, is getting the same preposterous treatment by Robert Spencer, in his book *Did Muhammad Exist?*). In this age of hyper-rationalist insanity, we have gone from the atheist who doesn't believe in God, which can be understandable on its own terms, to the crank who doesn't believe in historiography — and that isn't worth our serious consideration at all. So it's the case these days that not even *ordinary* evidence may be adequate for establishing *ordinary* claims. As Chesterton wrote in his classic little book *Orthodoxy,* "The madman is not the man who has lost his reason. He is the man who has lost everything except his reason."

Now, the paragraphs above may, paradoxically, come across like polemics and apologetics to the reader. I assure you, though, that they are not. For one thing, I am writing these things for Christians, not as an argument for non-Christians. If any non-Christians should read this, they can, if they choose, make of it what they will; but, with respect, I'm not writing to them. My contention here, aimed only at confessing Christians, is this: Engagement in polemics with non-Christians, regarding matters we hold to be sacred, is "good" for only two dubious results. It makes of the faith a systematic body of logical assertions and casuistic theories, and it makes of "God" and "Christ" merely the premises, articles, and conclusions of an intellectual dispute. As with dogmatism and biblicism above, it flattens the faith and complicates the teachings of Christ unnecessarily. Spiritually speaking, it's sterile. Related to that last remark, it distracts disciples from growing in the way of living which Jesus taught, depriving them of peace and charity, spoiling humility, and diverting the mind and heart from contemplative prayer.

II.

I would suggest what seems to me to be two corrective perspectives which we might adopt with benefit toward non-Christians who would draw us into controversies. I will venture out on a limb and assume here that we share a common vision among us of "mere Christianity" and "ecumenical orthodoxy."

The first perspective we should seek to acquire is that of *humility,* a humility that is intentionally the antithesis of defensiveness, or anger at being misrepresented or baited, or any sign of ecclesiastical triumphalism. One way to get that last temptation out of our system — that of triumphalism, usually involving the idea that our brand of Christianity is the "real" one or the "truest" version or "infallible," and so on — is to realize what a divided, combative lot we Christians have become after seventeen centuries of the Christendom model of church. I find myself in full agreement with the view expressed by Thomas Fleming, though perhaps for reasons other than those he might espouse. In an editorial for *Chronicles* some years ago, he wrote the following:

> The schisms that have divided Christ's body — as the soldiers divided His garments — are the worst scandals in Christendom, worse, by far, than dissolute popes, heretical sects, and the laxity of faith that is the chief characteristic of modern times. To obviate the usual arguments and exceptions, I am willing to believe most of what is said by all sides against each other: that Rome was poaching on Orthodox territories and inserting innovations into the creed, that the Byzantine Church had fallen under the sway of the emperor, that the Renaissance Church practiced the foulest abuses, that Luther was an egoist and oath-breaker. There is enough blame to go around, as there is in any marriage, and after the shame of a divorce it may be impossible to think clearly or speak honestly of

the ex-spouse — until, perhaps, one or both of them are dying. With Christendom in its death throes, I wonder if there is any chance of patching things up.[1]

All our churches stand guilty of words spoken and deeds done against each other, whatever glories there may also have been in their histories. In the matter of schism, as both a historical and a perpetuated reality, "they have all gone astray . . . there is none that does good, no, not one" (Rom. 3:12). If we can admit *that,* then we will have the humility that is appropriate, not only for dealing with one another, but for dealing with non-believers as well. Arrogance and divisiveness do not exhibit anything of the Spirit of Jesus Christ.

The other perspective that we should seek to cultivate is, for lack of a better term, what I will call an *eschatological perspective,* making it at once clear that my meaning has absolutely nothing to do with "end times" theories whatsoever. Eschatology, as popularly understood, doesn't interest me at all.

By an "eschatological perspective," I mean the opposite of spiritual myopia. I mean a perspective that is oriented to the future, one which is farsighted and sees the present, Western, post-Christendom condition of the church in light of the fact that "our commonwealth is in heaven, and from it we await a Savior, the Lord Jesus Christ" (Phil. 3:20), and that the *true* church is ultimately "the Jerusalem above [, which] is free, and she is our mother" (Gal. 4:26). In relationship to that eschatological church, we who are "in Christ" are together in the process of "growing into a holy temple in the Lord" (Eph. 2:21), whether we hail from, ecclesiastically speaking, the "elder

---

1. Thomas Fleming, "One World, One Leader, One God," *Chronicles: A Magazine of American Culture,* December 1998, p. 11.

Rome" (i.e., Rome), the "new Rome" (i.e., Constantinople), the "third Rome" (i.e., Moscow), or no Rome at all (i.e., the whole Protestant spectrum).

This might not sit well with some, but I'm confident to say that it accords well with the mind of the New Testament and the early church — that is to say, with what has been called the "Great Tradition" at its most pure. The eschatological perspective keeps in mind that the church on earth at its best is really an imperfect image of what will be fully realized and perfected in the future, when "the holy city, new Jerusalem" will come "down out of heaven from God, prepared as a bride adorned for her husband" (Rev. 21:2), "without spot or wrinkle or any such thing . . . holy and without blemish" (Eph. 5:27). Our role here and now, in light of that promise, is to be "the salt of the earth," "the light of the world," and "a city set on a hill . . . that [those without allegiance to the kingdom of heaven] may see [our] good works and give glory to [our] Father who is in heaven" (Matt. 5:13-16). The good news and glad tidings we have should be fully visible in the sorts of lives we lead and the communities we form. All the time we look to our goal, beyond this life and this age. We are proclaiming another kingdom, not trying to secure a place in the world's estimation through our clever polemics and incisive apologetics skills. Christendom, once again, is in its final death throes, and we are living in a world grown increasingly hostile to anything smacking of traditional Christianity. An eschatological perspective ever keeps in mind how imperative it is, in the language of Paul, "to keep Satan from gaining the advantage over us; for we are not" — or, at least, should not be — "ignorant of his designs" (2 Cor. 2:11).

The prophetic imagination of Vladimir Solovyov (1853-1900) might provide us insight into what I am calling an "eschatological perspective." His most memorable writing is a short piece of fiction called "A Short Story of the Anti-Christ."[2] Solovyov was ahead of his time, controversially testifying to the essential, ontological union of Christians, despite the historical schisms existing between them. This union, as we noted in the last chapter, subsists in Christ himself, in his body through baptism, and its being is not simply reducible to the historical churches.

"A Short Story of the Anti-Christ" tells how the genuine disciples in the churches reunite in the twenty-first century during the reign of the Anti-Christ. Compromised by well-chosen allurements offered by the world's ruler and his false prophet, the various churches are divided between genuine disciples and the mere adherents of religion — that is to say, between those who make of their allegiance to Christ's kingdom something that cannot be compromised, and those who have already compromised it with a deified state. Both sides of this division unite with other like-minded groups, the orthodox among themselves and the new religionists among themselves. There is a "double ecumenism" that occurs in the story, if you will. The orthodox believers from each of the three major streams, led and represented by Pope Peter II (Catholicism), the Elder John of Russia (Orthodoxy), and Professor Pauli (Protestantism), are finally seen together in the wilderness, following the cosmic sign of the "woman clothed with the sun." This is followed by Christ's return in glory, and a united Christianity, gathered with Peter, John, and Paul (the same three figures as above, but now unveiled as the original apostolic witnesses), is depicted as approaching Zion to greet him. It is a magnificent conclusion, reflecting a biblical sensibility and a vision of the imperfections of this age giving way ultimately to Christ's kingdom.

2. Vladimir Solovyov, *War, Progress, and the End of History: Three Conversations, Including a Short Story of the Anti-Christ,* Introduction by Czeslaw Milosz, Afterword by Stephan Hoeller (Hudson, N.Y.: Lindisfarne Press, 1990). See especially pp. 159-91.

The conclusion of Solovyov's story reminds us that our lives as disciples now are directly related to our eschatological hope. Ontologically we are deeply and radically one already, despite our disunity on a shallow level; eschatologically, too, we are one and undivided. The questions for us, as Christendom disappears, are these: Will we be one and undivided before the world in the present time — at least to the best of our abilities to live that vision out? Will we try to speak with one voice? Will we proclaim, more by deeds than by words, the gospel that there is another kingdom on this earth, and that it offers a better way — one of peace, forgiveness, charity, humility, sacrifice, uprightness, wisdom, and all the other perennial virtues — than what the kingdoms of this world have to offer? Will we place ourselves on the few sure creedal dogmas of our faith, neither more nor less, as expressed in the simple terms of the *regula fidei?* Will we educate ourselves to read our scriptures intelligently? Will we stop treating our sacraments as dividing lines, and start honoring them as true signs of ontological unity between ourselves and Christ? Will we make efforts to look like the church Jesus established, before attempting to argue with those who find our faith unconvincing and unappealing? Ours is not an argument, but a life to be promoted — and only in the way that life is lived openly will it be accepted as credible. This is a point that cannot be stressed enough. Christ's life, death, and resurrection are given flesh and blood as "evidence" through the witness of Christian lives.

Instead of engaging in polemicism, then, let us witness by a better way: through dedication to the way taught by Jesus, perseverance and repentance whenever we fail, humility at all times, charity toward one another in all our dealings (even in our theological exchanges), peace and wise restraint toward all others, especially toward those who are not followers of Jesus, and hope for a future that — like it or not — will put all things in

STRANGERS AND PILGRIMS ONCE MORE

their proper perspective and that we will inevitably share. Next to these, polemics with atheists and others achieve very little, and usually nothing at all. What "speaks" to them are our proclamation of God's self-emptying compassion and our good deeds that indicate the truth of that proclamation.

Let Paul be our guide. To the Corinthian church he wrote that Christ had sent him "to preach the gospel [literally, to "evangelize" or "proclaim glad tidings"], and not with eloquent wisdom [*sophia logou*], lest the cross of Christ be emptied of its power." He goes on to say that God has made Christ Jesus "our wisdom." And, keeping the "holy" things and "pearls" of our faith from doggish and swinish desecration, Paul tells us that "among the mature we do impart wisdom, although it is not a wisdom of this age or of the rulers of this age," because "the unspiritual man does not receive the gifts of the Spirit of God, for they are folly to him" (cf. 1 Cor. 1:17–2:16). In this, Paul is acknowledging that Christians have both an "exoteric" (outward) proclamation to the world, and an "esoteric" (inner) tradition which should be protected and not talked about freely — and certainly never debated — with secular non-Christians. In this conviction, he is also imitating Jesus' practice: "To you [disciples] has been given the secret [*mysterion*] of the kingdom of God, but for those outside everything is in parables" (Mark 4:11). Our deepest communal and personal spiritual beliefs we should share among ourselves. They are not cheap or common items, and they do not belong to the public at large.

III.

Whereas reticence — even silence — is the better policy with secular non-Christians regarding topics that require spiritual depth and sensitivity among the interlocutors, there should be a different attitude and another potential path of relating to non-Christians of other religions. In many cases it is our faith's deepest, "esoteric" elements that provide us with a bridge to understanding other faiths, precisely at an approximate level of religious practice among them. For decades now there have been effective and profound discussions between Christians and Buddhists, Sufis, Hindus, and others, with many points of contact, especially in areas of contemplative prayer and spirituality. Often it has been those in monastic life who have taken the lead, a significant fact which indicates that the level of connection has been that of shared mystical experience between Christianity and other faiths. Nor should this surprise us. It has long been a feature of Christian tradition that the eternal Word of God, who definitively took flesh in Jesus of Nazareth, was always at work in the universal consciousness of humanity "made in his image."

In his *Retractions* (I.13.3), for example, St. Augustine wrote, "That which today is called the Christian religion existed among the ancients, and has never ceased to exist from the origin of the human race, until the time when Christ himself came, and men began to call 'Christian' the true religion which already existed beforehand." That is a powerful and important idea which undergirds the value of interreligious dialogue, and other Early Church Fathers said much the same as Augustine. In the eighteenth century, William Law, the great English mystic, could similarly write, "The eternal Word or Son of God did not then first begin to be the Savior of the world when He was born in Bethlehem of Judea; but that Word which became man in the Virgin Mary did from the beginning of the world enter as a word of life, a seed of salvation, into the first father of mankind. . . . Hence it was so many eminent spirits, partakers of a divine life, have appeared in so many parts of the heathen world; glorious names, sons of wisdom, that shone as lights hung out by God in the midst of idolatrous darkness."[3]

Such daring statements as these were not really quite so daring when Augustine wrote, nor would they have been terribly surprising to the contemporaries of William Law thirteen centuries later. To quite a few Christians today, however, these statements might not be so familiar or welcome, and might produce anxiety over the "uniqueness" of Jesus Christ. (Admittedly, too, these sentiments would not have been agreeable to all Christians at all times and in all places in Christian history.) But this was an intellectual position vis-à-vis other philosophies and religions of which many — though not all — Church Fathers would have approved without misgiving. It was widespread enough during the patristic age both to adhere to the definitive realization of truth in the gospel of Jesus Christ and, at the same time, to maintain that the formerly "hidden" truth had been glimpsed, however dimly or clearly, in the spiritual aspirations and traditions of humankind. Obviously, for Augustine and other great Christian intellects, what was primarily in mind regarding this dimmer and more general realization of truth was the Greek and Roman philosophical heritage, but most likely it included some limited knowledge of Persian, Egyptian, and Indian traditions as well. It is not at all farfetched to think that they would have had no insurmountable difficulty accepting a notion of "perennial philosophy" or "perennial wisdom" or "perennial religion" (the latter two designations being advanced decades ago by Frithjof Schuon).[4] Or, to use the terminology of the eminent Christian

3. Quoted in *Ye Shall Know the Truth: Christianity and the Perennial Philosophy,* edited by Mateus Soares de Azevedo, with a foreword by William Stoddart (Bloomington: World Wisdom, Inc., 2005), p. 211.

4. A number of Schuon's works are readily available. The two that are best as introductions to his thought (admittedly controversial, but quite

scholar of world religions, Huston Smith, Augustine and others could well have affirmed the idea of a "universal grammar of religion."

This is the language of a worthwhile little volume based on a series of exchanges between Huston Smith and the philosopher Henry Rosemont Jr. (the latter an atheist — in the most respectable sense of that term — and an authority on Confucianism), which perhaps deserves our attention here.[5] It owes something to the linguistic studies of Noam Chomsky; and all three — Smith, Rosemont, and Chomsky — were in fact once colleagues at MIT. So, in the book, there is both a warm exchange between two old friends, and the "invisible presence," so to speak, of a third party, whose insights permeate the discussion throughout. And, if one reads closely, it is also possible to detect in the background, as well, our old friend William James (see Chapter Two), that indispensible figure for any appreciation of all religious studies that came after him.

Put simply, Noam Chomsky proposed that human beings learn their native languages and dialects to a great extent independently of their intelligence or motivation and without formal instruction. This fact, determined by intensive research in linguistics, indicates that structural dependence and other principles of Universal Grammar must be innate to the human mind, and therefore unlike the principles and rules of physics, chess, or geology, which must be formally taught. These principles are uniform throughout the species, which means that they could

worthwhile notwithstanding) are *The Essential Frithjof Schuon,* ed. Seyyed Hossein Nasr (Bloomington: World Wisdom, Inc., 2005); and *The Transcendent Unity of Religions,* with an introduction by Huston Smith (Wheaton, Ill.: Quest Books), 1984.

5. Henry Rosemont Jr. and Huston Smith, *Is There a Universal Grammar of Religion?* (Peru, Ill.: Open Court Publishing Co., 2008).

be ascertained just from a study of English or any other particular language. In other words, one can discover the universal
elements of grammar, which are innate to the human mind, by
studying any single language.

Furthermore, as Chomsky's research found, it appears to be
the case that environmental stimuli don't *shape* "our responses
in areas for which we have an innate mental capacity," such as
language, but rather that they *trigger* the responses.[6] This is illustrated by the nineteenth-century account of the first study ever
conducted on a feral child, the so-called "wild boy of Aveyron."
It was not the case that, like the fictional Mowgli or Tarzan, he
had learned an "animal language" in the wild (although he could
imitate their sounds); rather, he had learned no language at all.
Nothing in his environment had ever triggered his innate human
capacity for linguistics. The capacity was in him, in his brain, but
the human society needed for bringing it to life had been lacking.

What Huston Smith proposes is that the religious impulse in
man is likewise a "universal grammar" (and religion and linguistics are not the only innate capacities in the human mind). In the
book, he provides a detailed comparison of the world's six major religious traditions (Christianity, Judaism, Islam, Hinduism,
Buddhism, and the Chinese religious complex), showing how
they correspond conceptually both "exoterically" (outwardly, in
an ascending hierarchy toward the transcendent, ultimate reality) and "esoterically" (inwardly, in a descending hierarchy from
the body to the deepest point of the spirit or consciousness). In
other words, there is, across the full range of world religions, almost exact correspondences of perceptions of reality and levels
of being and consciousness between all the major faiths. Put an-

6. Rosemont Jr. and Smith, *Is There a Universal Grammar of Religion?*
Cf. pp. 71ff.

Saying Yes to Evangelism, and No to Polemicism

other way, bridges of understanding exist in the very structures of every religion, and the "worldviews" of them all, taken together, are remarkably congruent.[7]

So it is that, whereas dialogue with an ideological atheist or scientistic enthusiast, who is actively resistant to these concepts, is extremely difficult (due mainly to the obstreperous character of much religious–anti-religious dispute), profound dialogue between adepts or disciples of all faiths should be, and often is, much less difficult. There are natural points of contact between adherents of religion in general which do not exist between the religious and the anti-religious, because these innate capacities are actively denied by the latter. Religion may very well be a major factor in the promotion of peace in the world, and not a hindrance to it. In fact, if the twentieth century tells us anything about world conflicts, it is to beware of anti-religious zeal and movements. That's where the threat of carnage and horror has proved to be most virulent. (It should be noted here in passing that the majority of the world's wars have not been instigated by religion, as anti-religionists popularly maintain. In the *Encyclopedia of Wars,* the authors have shown that, out of a total of 1,763 wars, only 123 can be classified as actually religious in nature. That amounts to less than 7 percent of all wars ever fought.)[8]

The question that seems most pressing for Rosemont in the book, in response to Smith's proposal, is simply whether or not man's innate religious "grammar," seen in the parity of the world's various faiths, corresponds to an ontological reality. Smith would say it does (as might Augustine or Law, as well

7. Rosemont Jr. and Smith, *Is There a Universal Grammar of Religion?* See especially Smith's diagram on p. 13 and the discussion which follows.

8. Charles Phillips and Alan Axelrod, *Encyclopedia of Wars,* 3 vols. (New York: Facts on File, 2004).

as Schuon), but Rosemont remains unconvinced. Be that as it may, the Christian may well agree with Huston Smith. Each particular religion, then, reveals the same universal perspective of the nature of reality, both "inner" and "outer," "upward" and "downward." The innate capacity for religion is "triggered" by the practices and scriptures of each particular faith tradition, and, at their best, practitioners are led both toward the ultimate (or, as Smith is not afraid to say, God) and deeper, past the ego, into their truest and most compassionate selves.

Both Smith and Rosemont acknowledge, of course, the many evils perpetrated in the name of religion; but, in direct opposition to such pop atheists as Richard Dawkins, Sam Harris, and the like, they maintain both that religion has been a force for good in the world and that there is no serious possibility of its disappearing, any more than there is likely to be a cessation of language. It is Rosemont who rightly states the now-familiar pragmatic conclusion regarding the value of any religious tradition: "We should check the temptation to begin with 'What do [religions] believe?' and instead ask 'What do they do?' "

And here a Christian might also beneficially take to heart the insight of the great Hindu scholar of religions, and second president of India, Sarvepalli Radhakrishnan (1888-1975), who wrote the following in his classic study *Eastern Religions and Western Thought*:

> If the pagan world produces characters full of love and piety, we cannot say that any one religion contains all the truth or goodness that exists. The Psalmist exclaims: "This is the gate of the LORD: the righteous enter into it." "Of a truth," said the amazed St. Peter, "I perceive that God is no respecter of persons, but in every nation he that feareth Him, and worketh righteousness, is accepted of Him" [Acts 10:34]. The kind Samaritan is a believer in God according to

Jesus' declaration: "He that doeth the will of God, the same is my brother and my sister and my mother." The damnatory clauses of the Athanasian Creed are in direct opposition to the simple determination of discipleship which Jesus laid down. We must judge religious men, not by what they say, but by what they do.[9]

IV.

What does it mean, then, to proclaim the gospel, to "evangelize"?

To those with no religious background or commitment to speak of, the gospel should be direct, without complication, and without argumentativeness or polemics (which means that evangelizing should usually be left to those who have shown some maturity in their discipleship). It should come about naturally — never in a forced way. If someone wishes to turn the occasion into an argument, the discussion should be brought to a conclusion without falling into a quarrel, as well as that can be managed.

The emphasis should be on good news, not on morals. Christian morals are part of discipleship, and are only part of the gospel to the extent that most persons know that they have done things of which they are ashamed. Nor should there be an emphasis on heaven and hell. Regarding hell, the gospel is not that we must "receive Jesus" so that we can "go to heaven" when we die, and avoid "hell." That is to cheapen the message, and, in fact, that interpretation has no sound support from the New Testament. Our "going to heaven" after death, it should be noted, is not a New Testament idea. Rather, the apocalyptic and poetic im-

9. Sarvepalli Radhakrishnan, *Eastern Religions and Western Thought* (Oxford: Clarendon Press, 1939), p. 320.

age in the New Testament is almost the reverse — "heaven" coming down to earth. Similarly, when Jesus speaks of "Gehenna" (mistranslated as "hell"), it is always a metaphor, and always in conjunction with not living according to the right way of life. In effect, it is a pointed warning against throwing away one's true, spiritually fertile life. Jesus' language is not literal; and to understand "Gehenna" to mean a sort of geographical "place" to which one goes after death is to misread a powerful metaphor, suggestive of waste and loss, as literal descriptiveness. John's Gospel, in fact, "demythologizes" these concepts by contrasting "perishing" with "eternal life." The former word means, quite simply, ceasing to live; and "eternal life" in John refers exclusively to the life in God that Jesus has come to bestow abundantly, which begins in this life and extends beyond the limits of our physical existence. I have written elsewhere on this, so I won't belabor the subject further here.[10]

Nor is the proclamation of the gospel meant to be a Bible study. Quoting scripture should be sparing — we are not "preaching the Bible" but inviting persons to experience the mystery of God. We must never forget that there is a deep, profoundly mystical element of our faith, a discipline and a practice to which we point. We are inviting people to discipleship, not church attendance.

Some fundamental features of presentation might be these (note the careful language). There is a God. He is in all things and beyond all things. He made all things. He cannot be comprehended, but he has revealed himself to the extent that human limitations could take it in. He has been known throughout the ages. He can be experienced, and one can grow into deeper knowledge of God. Human beings are "fallen" — which means they know

---

10. See my book titled *Taking Jesus at His Word: What Jesus Really Said in the Sermon on the Mount* (Grand Rapids: Wm. B. Eerdmans, 2012), pp. 46-48.

failure, suffering, and death. Human beings were created to know God. Union with God overcomes the destructive aspects of existence, such as evil and death, so that they don't have the final say over our lives. To show us the way, God has come to us in Jesus Christ. To see Jesus is to see what God is like, in a way that we can understand him — as a human being among us. In Christ, God emptied himself and meets us where we are, no matter where we have strayed off the path — in our lives, in our failures and wrongdoings, in our sufferings, and even in our death. As low as we can sink — even to the grave — Christ has entered in and meets us there. He has so identified himself with us, out of love for us, that he has carried upon himself even our sins. They were crucified in his own flesh so that we might be free of them. By his resurrection, we have the promise of life in God. By his Holy Spirit (or Holy Breath), we can have deep inner knowledge of God and growth into our true purpose — to become by grace what Christ is by nature. We can live now in his kingdom. Christ is the world's judge; but we needn't fear because he is also our savior, advocate, and support. And when we fail (as we will), he will forgive and strengthen us, so that we can continue on with him. . . .

These are only suggestions; but the message needs to be clear and simple, without too much jargon, without threats, and with the stress put firmly on God's love, mercy, and generosity. Most importantly, the message must be backed up by the example of persons who endeavor consciously, but with humility (because everyone will stumble from time to time), to live according to the way that Jesus taught.

With those of other faiths, we have a somewhat different agenda in view, and, quite likely and realistically, another aim when sharing the good news. Since today we live in a world in which it isn't uncommon to rub elbows with sincere believers from many religious backgrounds (not unlike, in some ways, the world the first Christians inhabited), we should be prepared to learn what others believe religiously every bit as much as to share what we believe. This should cause us no fear or anxiety. After all, if Huston Smith is correct (and I, for one, believe he is), we all — both Christians and those of other faiths — share the "universal grammar of religion." Or, put another way, the everlasting Word of God has been active in the consciousness of all humanity from the beginning, shaping and directing it; and it is this same Word, we claim, who has revealed himself fully in Jesus Christ.

Perhaps we might use the classical triad of truth, beauty, and goodness as the measure of a religion's genuine worth. This is not at all an arbitrary standard, but one with a long and venerable heritage behind it. We are justified in assuming that, wherever these are present, we find the Word of God. If God cannot be found where truth, beauty, and goodness are found — wherever that may conceivably be — then God is not to be found. When we compare the enshrined teachings of the world's great religions, we find numerous correspondences between them in their ethics and spiritualities and their uses of ritual and scriptures. We soon discover that, along with obvious outward differences, there are also surprising similarities — a common "grammar," a common search, and a common acquisition of wisdom in those three inseparable elements of the ancient triad. Even in concepts which, at a superficial or preliminary inspection, appear to be mutually exclusive, those who go more patiently in open-minded study of other faiths will invariably find common ground experientially (for example, in meditation practices), and will also discover that even seemingly forbidding doctrines, cloaked in different words and systems, can begin to reveal a harmony between them (for example, the apophatic, or "negative," theology of Christian mystics and thinkers, such as Pseudo-Dionysius, Maximus the Confessor, Gregory Palamas, Meister Eckhart, the author of *The*

Cloud of Unknowing, John of the Cross, and others, and similar "apophatic" ideas in Hindu, Buddhist, Taoist, and Sufi thought).

During the last century especially, many fruitful dialogues have been achieved between the most adept spiritual practitioners of various religions, and these exchanges have revealed the deep-rooted commonality that exists. There, the Christian can and should believe, is the living point of contact between human consciousness and the universal revelation of the Word of God. What the gospel is in this context, then, is the assertion of the Christian that Jesus is that Word, come in human flesh and blood. Where Christ has left evidence of himself in the truth, beauty, and goodness of other faiths, there the Christian disciple should be glad, not resentful or troubled that, impossibly, Jesus' "uniqueness" may be compromised. (Does Jesus ever counsel us to be worried about this or any other matter?) Competition between religions is not what the gospel is about. Dialogue is an essential part of the gospel as we encounter the spirituality of other kinds of believers. We should have a relaxed, non-anxious, flexible freedom to recognize how the Word has disclosed himself to all in various hidden ways, and yet, as we believe, has shown himself definitively in Jesus. Those more committed to argument than to dialogue should be made to understand that argumentativeness does more harm to the reputation of the faith than good. Polemicism is always a sign of spiritual immaturity and insecurity, not a sign of authentic spiritual depth and worth.

In an interesting article written several years ago, historian Philip Jenkins tells of the interaction in Asia during the sixth, seventh, and eighth centuries between the (Nestorian) Church of the East, with its Semitic roots and Syriac language, and Oriental religions, and particularly of the meeting of Christian monks with missionaries of Mahayana Buddhism. "In this diverse world" of the East, stretching from Persia into China and India, writes Jenkins,

Buddhist and Christian monasteries were likely to stand side by side, as neighbors and even, sometimes, as collaborators. Some historians believe that Nestorian missionaries influenced the religious practices of the Buddhist religion then developing in Tibet. Monks spoke to monks.

In presenting their faith, Christians naturally used the cultural forms that would be familiar to Asians. They told their stories in the forms of sutras, verse patterns already made famous by Buddhist missionaries and teachers. A stunning collection of Jesus Sutras was found in caves at Dunhuang, in northwest China. Some Nestorian writings draw heavily on Buddhist ideas, as they translate prayers and Christian services in ways that would make sense to Asian readers. In some texts, the Christian phrase "angels and archangels and hosts of heaven" is translated into the language of buddhas and devas.

One story in particular suggests an almost shocking degree of collaboration between the faiths. In 782, the Indian Buddhist missionary Prajna arrived in Chang'an, bearing rich treasures of sutras and other scriptures. Unfortunately, these were written in Indian languages. He consulted the local Nestorian bishop, Adam, who had already translated parts of the Bible into Chinese. Together, Buddhist and Christian scholars worked amiably together for some years to translate seven copious volumes of Buddhist wisdom. Probably, Adam did this as much from intellectual curiosity as from ecumenical goodwill, and we can only guess about the conversations that would have ensued: Do you really care more about relieving suffering than atoning for sin? And your monks meditate like ours do?[11]

And, Jenkins reminds us in the article, "Christianity, for much of its history, was just as much an Asian religion as Buddhism.

11. Philip Jenkins, "When Jesus Met Buddha," *The Boston Globe,* Dec. 14, 2008. You can find this article online: http://www.boston.com/bostonglobe/ideas/articles/2008/12/14/when_jesus_met_buddha/.

Asia's Christian churches survived for more than a millennium, and not until the 10th century, halfway through Christian history, did the number of Christians in Europe exceed that in Asia."[12] What ended this golden era of Asian Christian witness was not, as some might suppose, syncretism or assimilation of Christianity with other faiths. Rather, national persecution, militant Islam, mass famine, and the Mongol invasions took their toll on the church in the thirteenth century. Jenkins's concluding paragraphs are so pertinent to this subject, and in fact so relevant to the overarching theme of this book, that I don't hesitate to quote them here:

> . . . We are used to the idea of Christianity operating as the official religion of powerful states, which were only too willing to impose a particular orthodoxy upon their subjects. Yet when we look at the African and Asian experience, we find millions of Christians whose normal experience was as minorities or even majorities within nations dominated by some other religion. Struggling to win hearts and minds, leading churches had no option but to frame the Christian message in the context of non-European intellectual traditions. Christian thinkers did present their message in the categories of Buddhism — and Taoism, and Confucianism — and there is no reason why they could not do so again. . . .
>
> Perhaps, in fact, we are looking at our history upside down. Some day, future historians might look at the last few hundred years of Euro-American dominance within Christianity and regard it as an unnatural interlude in a much longer story of fruitful interchange between the great religions.
>
> Consider the story told by Timothy, a patriarch of the Nestorian church. Around 800, he engaged in a famous debate with the Muslim

12. Jenkins, "When Jesus Met Buddha."

caliph in Baghdad, a discussion marked by reason and civility on both sides. Imagine, Timothy said, that we are all in a dark house, and someone throws a precious pearl in the midst of a pile of ordinary stones. Everyone scrabbles for the pearl, and some think they've found it, but nobody can be sure until day breaks.

In the same way, he said, the pearl of true faith and wisdom had fallen into the darkness of this transitory world; each faith believed that it alone had found the pearl. Yet all he could claim — and all the caliph could say in response — was that some faiths thought they had enough evidence to prove that they were indeed holding the real pearl, but the final truth would not be known in this world.

Knowing other faiths firsthand grants believers an enviable sophistication, founded on humility. We could do a lot worse than to learn from what we sometimes call the Dark Ages.[13]

Jenkins reminds us here that a successful Christianity did flourish outside Christendom for hundreds of years. Even though the Western imperial church condemned the Church of the East as "heretical" in the fifth century, that estimation of it is much different today; and what we now know of the history of those strained relations in the fifth century, with all the convoluted arguments and uncompromising ecclesiastical personalities of the time, shows that the rift was largely a misunderstanding of theological language — of "dogmatism" rather than sound, simple creedal dogma. At any rate, a model of dialogue between religions that we might beneficially look to today, as Jenkins here suggests, is that which occurred in the East, outside Western Christendom. In those much more irenic relations, marked by humility and reasonableness, we find a way for us to walk in the post-Christendom West of the future. We see in them, perhaps, the "universal gram-

13. Jenkins, "When Jesus Met Buddha."

mar of religion," which we can speak together with those of other faith convictions. We need not be apprehensive about syncretism; but we should be apprehensive about misrepresenting Christ through lack of humility, and refusing to see him hidden wherever truth, beauty, and goodness are being pursued and found.

Finally, pragmatically speaking, we should stand together with religious believers of every kind in today's Western world, with its many ideologically anti-religious voices. Religious faith itself is under pressure, not just any one religion. We need each other's support if we are to face the falsehoods, ugliness, and evils of a secularized, materialistic, scientistic, and anti-religious world. Our world has much in it that corrodes, corrupts, and crushes human life through violence and viciousness, and we cannot afford to turn our backs on any who seek the perennial ways of wisdom, even if their singular way is not our own.

CONCLUSION: PITCHING OUR TENTS AND PASSING THROUGH

As Christians stand on the other side of Christendom's long run of seventeen centuries, and we find ourselves strangers and pilgrims once more, we have before us a new opportunity. We can and should be hopeful, not discouraged. A sort of long "Babylonian Captivity" is finally over. We are perhaps still confused about where we will go from here — how we will rebuild our houses, what sort of makeshift communities we will live in with other disciples, how much of the good things we have inherited from Christendom we should bring along with us, and so forth. When the Jews returned from the original Babylonian Captivity, they brought with them the synagogue and the rabbinical tradition and collected the books of their greatest and most farsighted prophets. They came back, chastened certainly, but ready for renewed and deeper commitment to God. In some vaguely similar way, we might hope the same for ourselves.

We have many beautiful traditions and forms, art and music and architecture, saints and heroes, mystics and theologians, spirituality and scholarship — all from the great age of Christendom. What we shouldn't want, however, are the petty and paltry things: divisiveness, intellectual poverty, arrogance, triumphalism — and the list could go on. So, once again in summary, here are our affirmations and negations.

- Yes to dogma and creed and orthodoxy and a firm doctrinal tradition for our foundation; but no to dogmatism that divides, confuses, complicates, and has no pragmatic purpose.

147

- Yes to our holy Bible, with its grand story of evolving knowledge of the self-disclosing God, and its New Testament of apostolic testimony; but no to flat, fundamentalist, anti-intellectual, and spiritually deadening biblicism.

- Yes to sacramental unity, with baptism as our ontological union with the body of Christ, and communion as the covenant bond in his flesh and blood, and both as the sole property of the Lord who instituted them; but no to institutional and hierarchical abuse of the sacraments and their meaning — abuse that places barriers between believers with artificial excuses for doing so, and thus makes the sacraments signs of division instead of union.

- Yes to proclaiming the good news that the Word was made flesh in Jesus Christ, and that he has brought new life to a fallen world; but no to polemics that would turn these glad tidings into arguments and controversy, dishonoring Christ and his way in the process.

- Yes, above all, to Jesus Christ and the kingdom he proclaimed and the way of life he taught.

May these become convictions in our emerging communities as we find ourselves in a new cultural situation. Strangely, we are coming home after all, if in fact we are departing from a land — an age — of captivity. Christians are never more at home in this world than when they know themselves to be "passers-by," just passing through, pitching their tents, sojourning as nomads in time, here today and elsewhere tomorrow . . . strangers and pilgrims.